IN ASSOCIATION WITH

SQA

Hodder Gibson
Model Practice
Papers
WITH ANSWERS

PLUS: Official SQA Specimen Paper
With Answers

Higher for CfE
Modern Studies

2014 Specimen Question Paper
& Model Papers

HODDER
GIBSON
AN HACHETTE UK COMPANY

This book contains the official 2014 SQA Specimen Question Paper for Higher for CfE Modern Studies, with associated SQA approved answers modified from the official marking instructions that accompany the paper.

In addition the book contains model practice papers, together with answers, plus study skills advice. These papers, some of which may include a limited number of previously published SQA questions, have been specially commissioned by Hodder Gibson, and have been written by experienced senior teachers and examiners in line with the new Higher for CfE syllabus and assessment outlines, Spring 2014. This is not SQA material but has been devised to provide further practice for Higher for CfE examinations in 2015 and beyond.

Hodder Gibson is grateful to the copyright holders, as credited on the final page of the Answer Section, for permission to use their material. Every effort has been made to trace the copyright holders and to obtain their permission for the use of copyright material. Hodder Gibson will be happy to receive information allowing us to rectify any error or omission in future editions.

Hachette UK's policy is to use papers that are natural, renewable and recyclable products and made from wood grown in sustainable forests. The logging and manufacturing processes are expected to conform to the environmental regulations of the country of origin.

Orders: please contact Bookpoint Ltd, 130 Park Drive, Abingdon, Oxon OX14 4SE. Telephone: (44) 01235 827720. Fax: (44) 01235 400454. Lines are open 9.00–5.00, Monday to Saturday, with a 24-hour message answering service. Visit our website at www.hoddereducation.co.uk. Hodder Gibson can be contacted direct on: Tel: 0141 848 1609; Fax: 0141 889 6315; email: hoddergibson@hodder.co.uk

This collection first published in 2015 by
Hodder Gibson, an imprint of Hodder Education,
An Hachette UK Company
2a Christie Street
Paisley PA1 1NB

BrightRED   Hodder Gibson is grateful to Bright Red Publishing Ltd for collaborative work in preparation of this book and all SQA Past Paper, National 5 and Higher for CfE Model Paper titles 2014.

Typeset by PDQ Digital Media Solutions Ltd, Bungay, Suffolk NR35 1BY

Printed in the UK

A catalogue record for this title is available from the British Library

ISBN: 978-1-4718-3724-1

3 2 1

2016 2015

Introduction
Study Skills – what you need to know to pass exams!

Pause for thought

Many students might skip quickly through a page like this. After all, we all know how to revise. Do you really though?

Think about this:

"IF YOU ALWAYS DO WHAT YOU ALWAYS DO, YOU WILL ALWAYS GET WHAT YOU HAVE ALWAYS GOT."

Do you like the grades you get? Do you want to do better? If you get full marks in your assessment, then that's great! Change nothing! This section is just to help you get that little bit better than you already are.

There are two main parts to the advice on offer here. The first part highlights fairly obvious things but which are also very important. The second part makes suggestions about revision that you might not have thought about but which WILL help you.

Part 1

DOH! It's so obvious but …

Start revising in good time

Don't leave it until the last minute – this will make you panic.

Make a revision timetable that sets out work time AND play time.

Sleep and eat!

Obvious really, and very helpful. Avoid arguments or stressful things too – even games that wind you up. You need to be fit, awake and focused!

Know your place!

Make sure you know exactly **WHEN and WHERE** your exams are.

Know your enemy!

Make sure you know what to expect in the exam.

How is the paper structured?

How much time is there for each question?

What types of question are involved?

Which topics seem to come up time and time again?

Which topics are your strongest and which are your weakest?

Are all topics compulsory or are there choices?

Learn by DOING!

There is no substitute for past papers and practice papers – they are simply essential! Tackling this collection of papers and answers is exactly the right thing to be doing as your exams approach.

Part 2

People learn in different ways. Some like low light, some bright. Some like early morning, some like evening / night. Some prefer warm, some prefer cold. But everyone uses their BRAIN and the brain works when it is active. Passive learning – sitting gazing at notes – is the most INEFFICIENT way to learn anything. Below you will find tips and ideas for making your revision more effective and maybe even more enjoyable. What follows gets your brain active, and active learning works!

Activity 1 – Stop and review

Step 1

When you have done no more than 5 minutes of revision reading STOP!

Step 2

Write a heading in your own words which sums up the topic you have been revising.

Step 3

Write a summary of what you have revised in no more than two sentences. Don't fool yourself by saying, "I know it, but I cannot put it into words". That just means you don't know it well enough. If you cannot write your summary, revise that section again, knowing that you must write a summary at the end of it. Many of you will have notebooks full of blue/black ink writing. Many of the pages will not be especially attractive or memorable so try to liven them up a bit with colour as you are reviewing and rewriting. **This is a great memory aid, and memory is the most important thing.**

Activity 2 — Use technology!

Why should everything be written down? Have you thought about "mental" maps, diagrams, cartoons and colour to help you learn? And rather than write down notes, why not record your revision material?

What about having a text message revision session with friends? Keep in touch with them to find out how and what they are revising and share ideas and questions.

Why not make a video diary where you tell the camera what you are doing, what you think you have learned and what you still have to do? No one has to see or hear it, but the process of having to organise your thoughts in a formal way to explain something is a very important learning practice.

Be sure to make use of electronic files. You could begin to summarise your class notes. Your typing might be slow, but it will get faster and the typed notes will be easier to read than the scribbles in your class notes. Try to add different fonts and colours to make your work stand out. You can easily Google relevant pictures, cartoons and diagrams which you can copy and paste to make your work more attractive and **MEMORABLE**.

Activity 3 – This is it. Do this and you will know lots!

Step 1

In this task you must be very honest with yourself! Find the SQA syllabus for your subject (www.sqa.org.uk). Look at how it is broken down into main topics called MANDATORY knowledge. That means stuff you MUST know.

Step 2

BEFORE you do ANY revision on this topic, write a list of everything that you already know about the subject. It might be quite a long list but you only need to write it once. It shows you all the information that is already in your long-term memory so you know what parts you do not need to revise!

Step 3

Pick a chapter or section from your book or revision notes. Choose a fairly large section or a whole chapter to get the most out of this activity.

With a buddy, use Skype, Facetime, Twitter or any other communication you have, to play the game "If this is the answer, what is the question?". For example, if you are revising Geography and the answer you provide is "meander", your buddy would have to make up a question like "What is the word that describes a feature of a river where it flows slowly and bends often from side to side?".

Make up 10 "answers" based on the content of the chapter or section you are using. Give this to your buddy to solve while you solve theirs.

Step 4

Construct a wordsearch of at least 10 X 10 squares. You can make it as big as you like but keep it realistic. Work together with a group of friends. Many apps allow you to make wordsearch puzzles online. The words and phrases can go in any direction and phrases can be split. Your puzzle must only contain facts linked to the topic you are revising. Your task is to find 10 bits of information to hide in your puzzle, but you must not repeat information that you used in Step 3. DO NOT show where the words are. Fill up empty squares with random letters. Remember to keep a note of where your answers are hidden but do not show your friends. When you have a complete puzzle, exchange it with a friend to solve each other's puzzle.

Step 5

Now make up 10 questions (not "answers" this time) based on the same chapter used in the previous two tasks. Again, you must find NEW information that you have not yet used. Now it's getting hard to find that new information! Again, give your questions to a friend to answer.

Step 6

As you have been doing the puzzles, your brain has been actively searching for new information. Now write a NEW LIST that contains only the new information you have discovered when doing the puzzles. Your new list is the one to look at repeatedly for short bursts over the next few days. Try to remember more and more of it without looking at it. After a few days, you should be able to add words from your second list to your first list as you increase the information in your long-term memory.

FINALLY! Be inspired...

Make a list of different revision ideas and beside each one write **THINGS I HAVE** tried, **THINGS I WILL** try and **THINGS I MIGHT** try. Don't be scared of trying something new.

And remember – "FAIL TO PREPARE AND PREPARE TO FAIL!"

CfE Higher Modern Studies

The course

You will have studied the following three units:

- Democracy in Scotland and the United Kingdom
- Social Issues in the United Kingdom
- International Issues

Your teacher will usually have chosen one topic from each of the three sections above and you will answer questions on these in your exam (see table below).

Unit of the course	Option one	Option two
Democracy in Scotland and the UK	Democracy in Scotland	Democracy in the UK
Social Issues in the UK	Social Inequality	Crime and the Law
International Issues	World Powers	World Issues

Candidates are expected to complete three internal unit assessment items (part knowledge and understanding and part source-based). These must be completed to gain an overall course award.

The added value comes from the question paper and is an externally-marked assessment. This consists of two parts:

- Higher question paper

  60 marks allocated – two-thirds of marks
- Higher assignment

  30 marks allocated – one-third of marks

Total marks available = 90

The marks you achieve in the question paper and assignment are added together and an overall grade will be awarded. The grade is based on your total marks. Based on notional difficulty, 63 and above (70% and above) is an A; 54–62 (60%–69%) is a B; and 45–53 (50% to 59%) is a C.

The question paper

You will have 2 hours and 15 minutes to complete the question paper with a total of 60 marks allocated. There are three sections with each section worth 20 marks.

There are 16 marks available for skills-based questions and 44 marks for knowledge and understanding. These are assessed in three extended responses worth either 12 or 20 marks.

In the exam paper, more marks are awarded for knowledge and understanding than skills so it is crucial that you have a sound grasp of content.

Skills or source-based questions

There are two types of skills questions that you will have practised in class. Both are allocated 8 marks. These are:

1. Using up to three complex sources of information: **'to what extent is it accurate to state that...'**
2. Using up to three complex sources of information: **'what conclusions can be drawn...'**

As preparation for your exam, the best advice would be to practise source-based questions and to review the types of information required by an examiner for full marks. Remember, all the answers in source-based questions are contained within the sources. No marks are awarded for additional knowledge.

Knowledge (or extended response) questions

In the knowledge section of your exam you could be asked questions that have a similar style to the following:

- **Discuss – 20-mark extended response**, for example:

  The political system provides an effective check on the government.

  Discuss with reference to a world power you have studied.
- **To what extent – 20-mark extended response**, for example:

  To what extent has a world issue you have studied had an impact in different countries?
- **Evaluate – 12-mark extended response**, for example:

  One aim of an electoral system is to provide fair representation.

  Evaluate the effectiveness of an electoral system you have studied in providing fair representation.

  You should refer to electoral systems used in Scotland or the United Kingdom or both in your answer.
- **Analyse – 12-mark extended response**, for example:

  Analyse the different lifestyle choices that may result in poor health.

Remember, in your course exam the knowledge questions for the International Issues section will not refer to a particular country or issue. You will be expected to base your answer around your knowledge and understanding of the World Power or World Issue you have studied.

Remember, also, in your course exam the two skills-based questions may appear in any two of the three sections. There will be no choice offered for skills-based questions. For example, if a skills-based question is examined in the Social Issues section, it will either be based on Social Inequality or Crime and the Law. The question is testing your skills and no knowledge is needed to answer the question.

What makes a good extended response answer?

- One that answers the question and only provides knowledge and understanding and analysis/evaluation that is **relevant** to the question.
- One that is aware of the different requirements of a 20-mark and 12-mark answer. A 20-mark answer should include greater skills of analysis and evaluation and structured answer than in a 12-mark answer.
- One that uses **up-to-date, relevant** examples to illustrate your understanding of the question being asked.
- One that includes a range of points with detailed exemplification and explanation, and analysis/evaluation.
- For a 12-mark answer, one that includes knowledge/understanding and **either** analysis **or** evaluation. For a 20-mark response, one that includes knowledge/understanding, analysis, evaluation, a structure/line of argument and draws valid conclusions that address the question.

What makes a poor extended response answer?

- One that does not answer the question, or tries to change the question being asked. This is sometimes called "turning a question".
- One that gives detailed description or explanation that is not relevant to the question.
- One that contains information which is out of date.
- One that **only** provides a list of facts with no development or analysis/evaluation.

What makes a poor source-based answer?

- One that doesn't make use of all of the sources provided.
- One that fails to link information across sources.
- For the "objectivity" question, one that fails to make an overall judgement on the statement or fails to comment on the validity or reliability of the sources.
- For the "conclusions" question, one that fails to make an overall conclusion.

So you are now ready to answer the exam questions. Keep calm and don't panic.

Good luck!

HIGHER FOR CfE

2014 Specimen Question Paper

National
Qualifications
SPECIMEN ONLY

SQ32/H/01

Modern Studies

Date — Not applicable

Duration — 2 hours and 15 minutes

Total marks — 60

SECTION 1 — DEMOCRACY IN SCOTLAND AND THE UNITED KINGDOM—20 marks

Attempt Question 1 and EITHER Question 2(a) OR 2(b)

SECTION 2 — SOCIAL ISSUES IN THE UNITED KINGDOM—20 marks
    Part A Social inequality in the United Kingdom
    Part B Crime and the law in the United Kingdom

Attempt Question 1 and EITHER Question 2(a) OR 2(b) OR 2(c) OR 2(d)

SECTION 3 — INTERNATIONAL ISSUES—20 marks
    Part A World powers
    Part B World issues

Attempt EITHER Question 1(a) OR 1(b) OR 1(c) OR 1(d)

Write your answers clearly in the answer booklet provided. In the answer booklet, you must clearly identify the question number you are attempting.

Use **blue** or **black** ink.

Before leaving the examination room you must give your answer booklet to the Invigilator; if you do not, you may lose all the marks for this paper.

SECTION 1 — DEMOCRACY IN SCOTLAND AND THE UNITED KINGDOM — 20 marks

Attempt Question 1 and **EITHER** Question 2(a) **OR** 2(b)

Question 1

Study Sources A and B below and opposite then attempt the question that follows.

SOURCE A

The 2010 General Election televised debates

The 2010 General Election witnessed the first live television debates between leaders from each of the three main UK parties — Conservatives, Labour and the Liberal Democrats. Cameron, Brown and Clegg all hoped to visually connect with voters during a tightly fought campaign nicknamed the 'digital election'.

Before the first-ever debate of its kind, an Ipsos MORI poll revealed 60% of those voters surveyed felt the TV debates would be important to them in helping decide the way they would vote. The performance of the candidates during the debates could also have the potential to alter the way the media would handle coverage of each of the leaders and their parties. Following the debates, a range of polls suggested Nick Clegg had won convincingly, with many voters indicating they would switch to the Liberal Democrats. The success of Nick Clegg led to claims of 'Cleggmania' and a prediction of a historic increase in the number of seats for the Liberal Democrats.

A second survey conducted after the election by an independent polling organisation found the leaders' TV debates changed the voting intentions of more than a million voters. Put another way, the results indicated that the debates altered the voting behaviour of more than 4% of the electorate. Also, it could be argued that TV coverage of the leaders' debate motivated thousands of voters to use their vote when otherwise they may not have done. In some parts of the country there was a rise of 17% in younger voters indicating that they would turn out to vote. On the other hand, it could be argued that the TV debates only reinforced the existing views most people had.

A third survey from the British Election Study 2010 found 9.4m people watched the first live debate on ITV, 4.5m watched the second debate on Sky and 8.5m the final debate on the BBC. After the second debate, polling figures suggested Cameron and Clegg were joint winners. After the third debate, polling figures suggested Cameron was the winner. Overall, the results from this study appeared to suggest 12% of voters changed their mind about which party to vote for as a consequence of watching the TV election debates.

After the polling stations closed and the votes were counted, it was found that no one party had an overall majority in the House of Commons. The Conservatives obtained the largest share of the overall vote polling 36% (up 3.7% from 2005), Labour attracted 29% of the vote (down 6.2% from 2005) and the Liberal Democrats 23% (up 1% from 2005).

(Adapted from various sources)

MARKS

Section 1 Question 1 (continued)

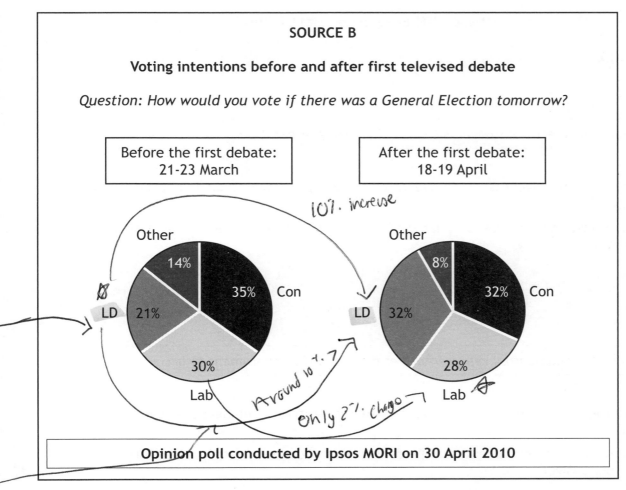

SOURCE B

Voting intentions before and after first televised debate

Question: How would you vote if there was a General Election tomorrow?

Before the first debate:
21-23 March

After the first debate:
18-19 April

107. increase

Other
14%
35% Con
LD 21%
30%
Lab

Other
8%
32% Con
LD 32%
28%
Lab

Around 10 %.

Only 2% chonge

Opinion poll conducted by Ipsos MORI on 30 April 2010

Attempt the following question, using **only** the information in Sources A and B opposite and above.

To what extent is it accurate to state that the televised debates had a significant impact on voting intentions?

8

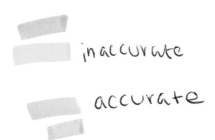 inaccurate

accurate

MARKS

Section 1 (continued)

Attempt **EITHER** Question 2(a) **OR** 2(b)

Question 2

(a)

One aim of an electoral system is to provide fair representation.

Evaluate the effectiveness of an electoral system you have studied in providing fair representation.

You should refer to electoral systems used in Scotland **or** the United Kingdom **or** both in your answer.

12

OR

(b)

One role of parliamentary representatives is to hold the government to account.

Evaluate the effectiveness of parliamentary representatives in holding the government to account.

You should refer to parliamentary representatives in Scotland **or** the United Kingdom **or** both in your answer.

12

SECTION 2 — SOCIAL ISSUES IN THE UNITED KINGDOM — 20 marks

MARKS

Attempt Question 1 and **EITHER** Question 2(a) **OR** 2(b) **OR** 2(c) **OR** 2(d)

Question 1

Study Sources A, B and C then attempt the question which follows.

SOURCE A

Social exclusion

Social exclusion is a term used to describe a person or group that lacks sufficient income to play a full part in society. For example, those socially excluded may not have enough money for special celebrations such as birthdays, for toys and books for children or for warm winter clothing. Those people experiencing social exclusion are most likely to be affected by low income, poor health, unemployment, fuel poverty and poor housing. The problems linked with social exclusion are something that both the Scottish and UK governments have been concerned to address in recent years.

Generally, although Scots are living longer, premature death and crime rates are falling and unemployment rates have also started to fall. However, social exclusion continues to impact on the lives of many Scottish citizens. The wealthiest groups in Scotland continue to lead better lives and the gap between the best and worst off in Scotland continues to widen.

Those who are worst off in Scottish society are less likely to access health services than those who are better off and usually have higher death and illness rates. Low life expectancy rates and long-term illness are often strong indicators of people experiencing social exclusion.

Evidence suggests that those people suffering social exclusion are not equally spread across Scotland. There are significant differences in health, earnings, crime and employment levels between Scottish local authorities and between urban and rural areas.

SOURCE B
Premature death rates for people under 65 years of age by selected Scottish local authority area per 100,000

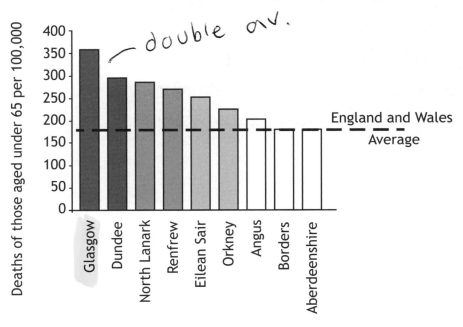

Section 2 Question 1 (continued)

SOURCE C

Social and economic data from selected
Scottish local authorities

Rural areas	Urban areas
Aberdeenshire	**Dundee City**
• Average gross earnings per week: £570·60 • Unemployment rate: 1·5% • Crime rate per 10,000 people: 286 • Employment rate: 79·6% • Life expectancy: 78·2 years • Long-standing illness: 11% • National percentage share of the poorest parts of the country: 0%	• Average gross earnings per week: £483·30 • Unemployment rate: 5·9% • Crime rate per 10,000 people: 616 • Employment rate: 68·4% • Life expectancy: 73·9 years • Long-standing illness: 17% • National percentage share of the poorest parts of the country: 5·8%
Borders	**Glasgow City**
• Average gross earnings per week: £430·11 • Unemployment rate: 3·3% • Crime rate per 10,000 people: 281 • Employment rate: 73·1% • Life expectancy: 77·5 years • Long-standing illness: 12% • National percentage share of the poorest parts of the country: 0·3%	• Average gross earnings per week: £506 • Unemployment rate: 5·8% • Crime rate per 10,000 people: 889 • Employment rate: 63·8% • Life expectancy: 71·6 years • Long-standing illness: 22% • National percentage share of the poorest parts of the country: 45%

(handwritten annotation: 7 years almost)

Attempt the following question, using **only** the information in Sources A, B and C opposite and above.

What conclusions can be drawn about social exclusion in Scotland?

You must draw conclusions about:

- the links between social exclusion and health
- the links between social exclusion and local authority area

You must give an overall conclusion on social exclusion in Scotland.

8

MARKS

Section 2 (continued)

Attempt **EITHER** Question 2(a) **OR** 2(b) **OR** 2(c) **OR** 2(d)

Question 2

Part A: Social inequality in the United Kingdom

Answers may refer to Scotland **or** the United Kingdom **or** both.

(a) Analyse government policies to tackle inequalities that affect a group in society.   **12**

OR

(b) Analyse the different lifestyle choices that may result in poor health.   **12**

OR

Part B: Crime and the law in the United Kingdom

Answers may refer to Scotland **or** the United Kingdom **or** both.

(c) Analyse government policies to tackle crime.   **12**

OR

(d) Analyse the ways in which the victims of crime are affected.   **12**

MARKS

SECTION 3 — INTERNATIONAL ISSUES — 20 marks

Attempt **EITHER** Question 1(a) **OR** 1(b) **OR** 1(c) **OR** 1(d)

Question 1

Part A: World powers

(a) *The political system provides an effective check on the government.*

Discuss with reference to a world power you have studied.   **20**

OR

(b) To what extent does a world power you have studied have influence in international relations?   **20**

OR

Part B: World issues

(c) *International organisations have been successful in resolving a significant world issue.*

Discuss with reference to a world issue you have studied.   **20**

OR

(d) To what extent has a world issue you have studied had an impact in different countries?   **20**

[END OF SPECIMEN QUESTION PAPER]

HIGHER FOR CfE

Model Paper 1

Whilst this Model Practice Paper has been specially commissioned by Hodder Gibson for use as practice for the Higher (for Curriculum for Excellence) exams, the key reference document remains the SQA Specimen Paper 2014.

National
Qualifications
MODEL PAPER 1

Modern Studies

Duration — 2 hours and 15 minutes

Total marks — 60

SECTION 1 — DEMOCRACY IN SCOTLAND AND THE UNITED KINGDOM—20 marks

Attempt Question 1 and **EITHER** Question 2(a) **OR** 2(b)

SECTION 2 — SOCIAL ISSUES IN THE UNITED KINGDOM—20 marks
        Part A Social inequality in the United Kingdom
        Part B Crime and the law in the United Kingdom

Attempt Question 1 and **EITHER** Question 2(a) **OR** 2(b) **OR** 2(c) **OR** 2(d)

SECTION 3 — INTERNATIONAL ISSUES—20 marks
        Part A World powers
        Part B World issues

Attempt **EITHER** Question 1(a) **OR** 1(b) **OR** 1(c) **OR** 1(d)

Write your answers clearly in the answer booklet provided. In the answer booklet, you must clearly identify the question number you are attempting.

Use **blue** or **black** ink.

Before leaving the examination room you must give your answer booklet to the Invigilator; if you do not, you may lose all the marks for this paper.

SECTION 1 — DEMOCRACY IN SCOTLAND AND THE UNITED KINGDOM — 20 marks

Attempt Question 1 and **EITHER** Question 2(a) **OR** 2(b)

Question 1

Study Sources A, B and C then answer the question that follows.

SOURCE A

2014 European Election Results in Great Britain

In May 2014, the United Kingdom elected 72 MEPs (59 from England) using a proportional representation system of voting. Nigel Farage, the leader of the United Kingdom Independence Party (UKIP), declared the result "an earthquake in British politics" and that UKIP was now "a truly national force" after it won the most votes and seats in the UK European Parliament elections.

The UKIP performance was impressive. UKIP increased its votes from the 2.49 million it had received in 2009 to 4.37 million. UKIP topped the poll in six of the nine regions of England with one of its strongest performances coming in the South-East where it doubled its MEPs to four. UKIP also increased its votes in Scotland and Wales. In Scotland, UKIP received 10.4% of the votes, but more importantly it gained its first ever Scottish MEP and retained its Welsh seat.

Labour recovered from its poor showing of 2009 when only 11 of its MEPs were elected and narrowly beat the Conservatives to second place with 25.4 % of the national votes. Its best performance was in London where it increased its share of the vote from 21.7% to 36.7%

The Conservatives, who had been the largest UK party in the 2009 elections, lost support to UKIP. It lost seven MEPs and was reduced to being the third largest party with 24% of the votes. The Conservative leader, David Cameron, claimed that the public was disillusioned with the EU.

For the Liberal Democrats, it was another disastrous performance. Almost one million of their 2009 voters deserted the party resulting in it losing ten of their 11 MEPs. The Liberal Democrat leader Nick Clegg has said he will not resign despite calls from within his party for his resignation.

While Scotland followed some of the national trends, it has its own political dimension. The SNP once again had the most votes. It returned two MEPs which was the same as in 2009. The Liberal Democrats lost their European seat and suffered a decline in votes. Labour retained its two seats with the Conservatives retaining their one seat and UKIP received the remaining one seat.

Adapted from various newspapers

Section1 Question1 (continued)

**SOURCE B — European Parliament Election Results 2014:
Great Britain (excluding Scotland)**

Party	% of vote	% change from 2009	Number of MEPs	Change +/-
Conservatives	23.9	− 3.8	18	− 7
Labour	25.4	+ 9.7	18	+ 7
Liberal Democrats	6.9	− 6.9	1	− 9
UKIP	27.5	+ 11.0	23	+ 11
Green Party	7.9	− 0.7	3	+ 1
Plaid Cymru	0.7	− 0.1	1	0

SOURCE C — European Parliament Election Results 2014: Scotland

Party	% of vote	% change from 2009	Number of MEPs	Change +/-
Conservatives	17.2.	+ 0.4	1	0
Labour	26.0	+ 5.1	2	0
Liberal Democrats	7.0	− 4.4	0	− 1
UKIP	10.4	+ 5.2	1	+ 1
SNP	29.0	− 0.1	2	0
Green Party	7.9	− 0.8	0	0

Attempt the following question, using **only** the information in Sources A, B and C opposite and above.

What conclusions can be drawn from the results of the 2014 European Elections?

You must draw conclusions about:

- the success of UKIP
- the success of other parties

You must give an overall conclusion on the results of the 2014 European Elections in Great Britain.

8

MARKS

Section 1 (continued)

Attempt **EITHER** Question 2(a) **OR** 2(b)

Question 2

(a)

One role of parliamentary representatives is to scrutinise government.

Evaluate the effectiveness of parliamentary representatives in scrutinising government.

You should refer to parliamentary representatives in Scotland **or** the United Kingdom **or** both in your answer.

12

OR

(b)

Some factors are more important in influencing voting behaviour than others.

Evaluate the importance of a range of factors that influence voting behaviour.

You should refer to recent elections held in Scotland **or** the United Kingdom **or** both in your answer.

12

SECTION 2 — SOCIAL ISSUES IN THE UNITED KINGDOM — 20 marks

Attempt Question 1 and **EITHER** Question 2(a) **OR** 2(b) **OR** 2(c) **OR** 2(d)

Question 1

Study Sources A, B and C then attempt the question which follows.

Source A: Views of selected Scottish groups on Minimum Unit Pricing (MUP) of Alcohol

The Alcohol (Minimum Pricing) (Scotland) Act 2012 passed by the Scottish Parliament introduced statutory minimum unit pricing (MUP) for alcohol, initially at 50p per unit. The SNP Government argues that minimum unit pricing of alcohol is needed to tackle alcohol abuse in Scotland. The law should have come into force in April 2013, however its legality has been challenged by the Scotch Whisky Association (SWA) and the European courts will decide.

SNP deputy leader Nicola Sturgeon stated: "For too long, too many Scots have been drinking themselves into an early grave. It is no coincidence that as the affordability of alcohol has plummeted in recent decades, alcohol-related deaths have increased." The SNP claims that MUP would lead to 1,200 fewer hospital admissions. Health indicators highlight that areas of deprivation have witnessed the highest increase in chronic liver disease (associated with abuse of alcohol). In 1993 alcohol-related deaths per 100,000 in the most wealthy area was 3 compared to 14 in the most deprived area. By 2003 it stood at 5 and 53 respectively. Areas with high levels of deprivation such as Glasgow and Greenock have poorer health compared to more wealthy areas such as Aberdeenshire and Eastwood.

The medical profession supports MUP and calls on the Scotch Whisky Association to drop its opposition to the bill. Doctors accept that there has been a reduction in hospital admissions and alcohol-related deaths. However alcohol is still a huge health and social problem for Scotland. The British Medical Association (BMA) argues that reducing the sale of ultra-cheap alcohol through minimum pricing will make a genuine lasting difference to health and improve the well-being of the Scottish public.

The SWA and its members argue that they are committed to tackling alcohol misuse and support responsible options. Minimum unit pricing, they argue, is an unfair and untargeted policy that penalises responsible drinkers, especially those on lower income. Their view is that there is no concrete evidence to support the claims made regarding the reduction in hospital admissions. Present action by the Scottish Government is already having an impact with the number of alcohol-related deaths in Scotland falling from over 1,500 in 2003 to just over 1,200 in 2012. Again alcohol-related hospital admissions have declined over recent years — so MUP is not necessary.

Adapted from various sources

Section 2 Question 1 (continued)

SOURCE B

General acute inpatient hospital admissions and discharges with an alcohol-related diagnosis: Scotland 2007/08 – 2011/12

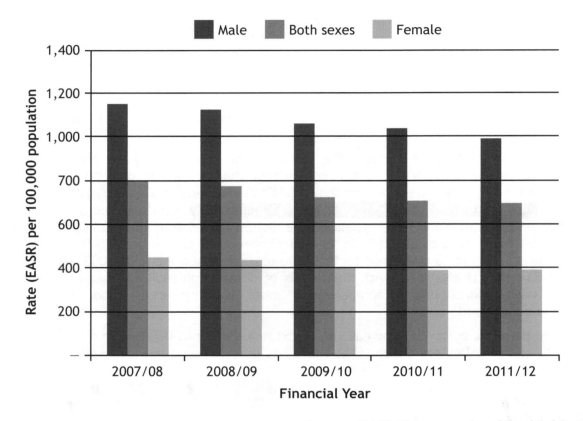

Source: EASR (European Age Standard Rate)

SOURCE C

Source C: Alcohol-related deaths rates per 100,000 of population (selected areas) 2012

AREA	Number of deaths
Aberdeenshire	12
Dumbarton	41
Dundee East	46
Eastwood East Renfrewshire	11
Glasgow Maryhill	56
Glasgow Shettleston	76
Greenock and Inverclyde	49
Paisley South	38

Source: Office for National Statistics (ONS) 2014

MARKS

Section 2 Question 1 (continued)

Use **only** the information in Source A, B and C to answer the following question.

To what extent is it accurate to state that minimum unit pricing (MUP) is needed to reduce alcohol-related problems in Scotland?

8

INACCURATE

ACCURATE

MARKS

Section 2 (continued)

Attempt **EITHER** Question 2(a) **OR** 2(b) **OR** 2(c) **OR** 2(d)

Question 2

Part A: Social inequality in the United Kingdom

Answers may refer to Scotland or the United Kingdom or both.

(a)   Analyse the consequences of social inequality on a group you have studied.   **12**

OR

(b)   Analyse government policies which aim to reduce social inequality.   **12**

OR

Part B: Crime and the law in the United Kingdom

Answers may refer to Scotland or the United Kingdom or both.

(c)   Analyse policies which aim to reduce re-offending.   **12**

OR

(d)   Analyse the consequences of crime on society.   **12**

MARKS

SECTION 3 — INTERNATIONAL ISSUES — 20 marks

Attempt **EITHER** Question 1(a) **OR** 1(b) **OR** 1(c) **OR** 1(d)

Question 1

Part A: World powers

(a) To what extent do individuals or groups in a world power you have studied experience social and economic inequality?   **20**

OR

(b)

The political system guarantees and protects the rights of all of its citizens.

Discuss with reference to a world power you have studied.   **20**

OR

Part B: World issues

(c)

An international issue can be caused by a range of political, social and economic factors.

Discuss with reference to a world issue you have studied.   **20**

OR

(d) To what extent has a world issue you have studied been solved by international organisations?   **20**

[END OF MODEL PAPER 1]

Model Paper 2

Whilst this Model Practice Paper has been specially commissioned by Hodder Gibson for use as practice for the Higher (for Curriculum for Excellence) exams, the key reference document remains the SQA Specimen Paper 2014.

HODDER
GIBSON
LEARN MORE

National Qualifications
MODEL PAPER 2

Modern Studies

Duration — 2 hours and 15 minutes

Total marks — 60

SECTION 1 — DEMOCRACY IN SCOTLAND AND THE UNITED KINGDOM—20 marks

Attempt Question 1 and **EITHER** Question 2(a) **OR** 2(b)

SECTION 2 — SOCIAL ISSUES IN THE UNITED KINGDOM—20 marks
      Part A Social inequality in the United Kingdom
      Part B Crime and the law in the United Kingdom

Attempt **EITHER** Question 1(a) **OR** 1(b) **OR** 1(c) **OR** 1(d)

SECTION 3 — INTERNATIONAL ISSUES—20 marks
      Part A World powers
      Part B World issues

Attempt Question 1 and **EITHER** Question 2(a) **OR** 2(b) **OR** 2(c) **OR** 2(d)

Write your answers clearly in the answer booklet provided. In the answer booklet, you must clearly identify the question number you are attempting.

Use **blue** or **black** ink.

Before leaving the examination room you must give your answer booklet to the Invigilator; if you do not, you may lose all the marks for this paper.

SECTION 1 – DEMOCRACY IN SCOTLAND AND THE UNITED KINGDOM – 20 marks

Attempt Question 1 and **EITHER** Question 2(a) **OR** 2(b)

Question 1

Study Sources A, B and C below and opposite then attempt the question that follows.

SOURCE A

Female Representation in Scottish and UK Politics

At the 2010 UK General Election 144 women Members of Parliament (MPs) were elected to the UK Parliament from 650 MPs. Between 2010 and 2014, after a series of by-elections, this number increased to 147 female MPs. Today almost 1 in 4 MPs are female compared to less than 1 in 10 in 1992.

Outside the House of Commons, around a quarter of the members of the House of Lords are women. In the National Assembly for Wales just over 40% of the representatives are female although this is down from around half of the Assembly Members (AMs) 15 years ago when the Welsh Assembly was established. In the European Parliament 40% of the UK Members of the European Parliament (MEPs) are women. In local government the number of female councillors has remained static at around 22% for a number of years.

In the Scottish Parliament women make up around a third of the Members of the Scottish Parliament (MSPs). In April 2014, 45 of the 129 MSPs were female. Disappointingly, this number is lower than when the Scottish Parliament was established in 1999 when 48 of the 129 MSPs were female.

Across the UK the main political parties have different levels of female representation. The Labour Party in Scotland and the UK has, for many years, had a policy of trying to return more women representatives, particularly women MPs. Recently, Labour's Deputy Leader Harriet Harman defended the party's use of all-female party candidate shortlists as the only way to stop the UK Parliament being dominated by men. She added that all other attempts to increase female representation in the UK Parliament 'had failed'. Labour first backed all-women shortlists in 1993.

The Conservative Party and the Liberal Democrat Party claim they would like to see more women representatives elected in their respective parties. However, many Conservative Party local associations oppose women-only shortlists, preferring to persuade more women to stand as candidates. The Liberal Democrats are opposed to women-only shortlists.

In Scotland, the Scottish National Party (SNP) and the Scottish Government now led by former deputy First Minister Nicola Sturgeon. In the Scottish Government, around 40% of Ministers are female. This is the highest female Scottish Cabinet representation since the Scottish Parliament was set up. At the SNP party conference in 2014, Ms Sturgeon stated she wanted to see something closer to half the Ministers in the Scottish Cabinet as female with half the MSPs also women. However, the percentage of SNP MSPs who are female has fallen from over 40% in 1999 to under 30% at the 2011 Scottish Parliament election.

MARKS

Section1 Question1 (continued)

SOURCE B — Male and Female Representation in UK and Scottish Parliaments

UK

Election Year	Male MPs	%	Female MPs	%
1997	539	82.9	120	18.2
2001	541	82.0	118	17.9
2005	521	80.6	127	19.3
2010	505	77.8	144	22.3

Scotland

Election Year	Male MSPs	%	Female MSPs	%
1999	81	64.0	48	36.0
2003	78	60.5	51	39.5
2007	86	66.6	43	33.4
2011	84	65.1	45	34.9

SOURCE C — Female MPs and MSPs by Party 2014

	Number					Percentage of party total			
Party (UK)	Lab	Con	Lib Dem	Other		Lab	Con	Lib Dem	Other
MPs	86	48	7	6		33	16	13	18

	Number					Percentage of party total			
Party (Scotland)	Lab	Con	Lib Dem	SNP		Lab	Con	Lib Dem	SNP
MSPs	17	6	1	18		46	40	20	26

Attempt the following question, using **only** the information in Sources A, B and C opposite and above.

What conclusions can be drawn about the representation of women in Scottish and UK politics?

You must draw conclusions about:

- the representation of women in the Scottish Parliament compared to the UK Parliament
- the representation of women in different political parties in Scotland and the UK

You must give an overall conclusion about the representation of women in politics.

8

Section 1 (continued)

Attempt **EITHER** Question 2(a) **OR** 2(b)

Question 2

(a)

> *Social class is an important factor influencing voting behaviour.*

Evaluate the importance of social class as a factor influencing voting behaviour.

You should refer to recent elections held in Scotland or the United Kingdom or both in your answer.

12

OR

(b)

> *Parliamentary representatives have a number of important roles in the decision-making process.*

Evaluate the importance of the different roles carried out by parliamentary representatives in the decision-making process.

You should refer to parliamentary representatives in Scotland or the United Kingdom or both in your answer.

12

SECTION 2 — SOCIAL ISSUES IN THE UNITED KINGDOM — 20 marks

MARKS

Attempt **EITHER** Question 1(a) **OR** 1(b) **OR** 1(c) **OR** 1(d)

Question 1

Part A: Social inequality in the United Kingdom

Answers may refer to Scotland or the United Kingdom or both.

(a)   To what extent is poverty the most important factor influencing health?   **20**

OR

(b)   *Government is failing to meet the aims of the Welfare State.*
    Discuss.   **20**

OR

Part B: Crime and the law in the United Kingdom

Answers may refer to Scotland or the United Kingdom or both.

(c)   To what extent is poverty the main cause of criminal behaviour?   **20**

OR

(d)   *Community-based punishments are more effective than prison in reducing re-offending.*
    Discuss.   **20**

SECTION 3 — INTERNATIONAL ISSUES — 20 marks

Attempt Question 1 and **EITHER** Question 2(a) **OR** 2(b) **OR** 2(c) **OR** 2(d)

Question 1

Study Sources A, B and C then answer the question that follows.

SOURCE A

Outstanding Victory for Obama in 2012 USA Presidential Election

The president of the USA is not chosen directly by the US people. Instead, presidents are elected by "electors" who are chosen by popular vote on a state-by-state basis. These "electors" then award their states' Electoral College votes (in most cases) to the candidate with the greatest support in their state.

The number of Electoral College votes in each state depends on the size of the state. For example, Florida, which has a large population (19.5m), receives 29 Electoral College votes compared to the three received by Vermont which has a small population (0.6m). There are 538 Electoral College votes in total. However, the popular votes achieved in a state are not shared proportionally between the leading candidates. In the 2012 presidential election in Florida, Barack Obama won 49.9% of the popular vote compared to 49.0% for Mitt Romney, yet Obama received all of the 29 Electoral College votes.

In 2008, the Democratic Party candidate Barack Obama made history by becoming the first African-American president of the United States. Obama secured victory with the highest ever recorded popular vote of 66,882,230 popular votes and won 365 Electoral College votes compared to the Republican candidate's 173 Electoral College votes.

The two major political parties are the Democratic Party and the Republican Party. There are other political parties which participate in presidential elections and in 2012, five other presidential candidates took part. In total these candidates gained less than 2% of the votes. A Democratic Party spokesperson stated that Obama once again had an outstanding election victory in both the Electoral College and popular vote. In particular, he had huge support from a wide range of groups in society especially the young, poor groups and those from an ethnic minority background. In 2012, Obama received 332 Electoral College votes compared to 206 for Romney. Obama also won 65,918,507 popular votes compared to Romney's 60,934,407.

Romney's main support came from the old, the rich and white voters. He won the popular vote in 24 of the 50 states and had narrow defeats in four states. If he had won these four states, it would have given Romney 270 Electoral College votes to Obama's 268 — and the Presidency. One of Obama's largest victories was in Hawaii where he gained just over 70% of the popular votes.

Adapted from BBC News website, November 2012

Section 3 (continued)

SOURCE B

Voting by age, income, religion and ethnicity in 2012 Presidential Election (%)

Age (Years)

	18–29	30–49	50–64	65+
Obama	60	52	47	44
Romney	38	47	52	56

Income

	Up to $49,999	$50,000–99,999	$100,000–199,999	Over $200,000
Obama	60	46	44	45
Romney	38	52	54	53

Religion

	Protestant	Catholic	Jewish	Mormons
Obama	43	50	69	21
Romney	56	48	30	78

Ethnicity

	White	African–American	Hispanic/Latino	Asian
Obama	39	93	71	73
Romney	59	6	27	26

Source: National Election Pool, a consortium of ABC News, Associated Press, CBS News, CNN, Fox News and NBC News

MARKS

Section 3 (continued)

SOURCE C

US Presidential Results 2012: Popular (millions) and Electoral College (%)

Party and Candidate*	Popular Vote 2012	Popular Vote 2008
Democrats: Obama	51.0%	52.9%
Republican: Romney	47.1%	45.6%

Electoral College	2012	2008
Democrats	61.7%	67.8%
Republican	38.3%	32.2%

Adapted from BBC News website November 2012

Obama was the Democrat candidate for both the 2008 and 2012 presidential elections. Romney was the Republican candidate in 2012 and McCain the candidate in 2008.

Use **only** the information in Source A, B and C to answer the following question.

To what extent is it accurate to state that the result of the 2012 USA Presidential Election was "an outstanding victory for Obama"?

8

ACCURATE

INACCURATE

MARKS

Section 3 (continued)

Attempt **EITHER** Question 2(a) **OR** 2(b) **OR** 2(c) **OR** 2(d)

Question 2

Part A: World powers

(a)   Analyse the international influence of a world power you have studied.   12

OR

(b)   Analyse policies implemented by government to solve a socio-economic issue in a world power you have studied.   12

OR

Part B: World issues

(c)   Analyse the actions taken by international organisations to resolve a world issue you have studied.   12

OR

(d)   Analyse the consequences of a world issue you have studied on those affected.   12

[END OF MODEL PAPER 2]

Model Paper 3

Whilst this Model Practice Paper has been specially commissioned by Hodder Gibson for use as practice for the Higher (for Curriculum for Excellence) exams, the key reference document remains the SQA Specimen Paper 2014.

National Qualifications MODEL PAPER 3

Modern Studies

Duration — 2 hours and 15 minutes

Total marks — 60

SECTION 1 — DEMOCRACY IN SCOTLAND AND THE UNITED KINGDOM—20 marks

Attempt **EITHER** Question 1(a) **OR** 1(b)

SECTION 2 — SOCIAL ISSUES IN THE UNITED KINGDOM—20 marks
　　　　Part A Social inequality in the United Kingdom
　　　　Part B Crime and the law in the United Kingdom

Attempt Question 1 and **EITHER** Question 2(a) **OR** 2(b) **OR** 2(c) **OR** 2(d)

SECTION 3 — INTERNATIONAL ISSUES—20 marks
　　　　Part A World powers
　　　　Part B World issues

Attempt Question 1 and **EITHER** Question 2(a) **OR** 2(b) **OR** 2(c) **OR** 2(d)

Write your answers clearly in the answer booklet provided. In the answer booklet, you must clearly identify the question number you are attempting.

Use **blue** or **black** ink.

Before leaving the examination room you must give your answer booklet to the Invigilator; if you do not, you may lose all the marks for this paper.

MARKS

SECTION 1 — DEMOCRACY IN SCOTLAND AND THE UNITED KINGDOM — 20 marks

Attempt **EITHER** Question 1(a) **OR** 1(b)

Question 1

(a)

Electoral systems do not always provide for fair representation.

Discuss.

You should refer to electoral systems used in Scotland or the United Kingdom or both in your answer.

20

OR

(b)

To what extent are pressure groups effective in influencing government decision making?

You should refer to pressure groups in Scotland or the United Kingdom or both in your answer.

20

SECTION 2 — SOCIAL ISSUES IN THE UNITED KINGDOM — 20 marks

Attempt Question 1 and **EITHER** Question 2(a) **OR** 2(b) **OR** 2(c) **OR** 2(d)

Question 1

Study Sources A, B and C then attempt the question that follows.

SOURCE A

Police Stop and Search Factfile — Scotland, England and New York City

- Two forms of Stop and Search powers are used by Scottish police officers: statutory search powers require reasonable suspicion that the person is concealing illegal possession; non-statutory search powers require the agreement of the individual to be stopped and searched. In England only statutory search powers are used. In New York City (NYC), Stop and Search is known as the Stop, Question and Frisk policy.

- The use of Stop and Search has widened across all areas of Scotland following the creation of Police Scotland in April 2013. Some local authority areas, such as Fife, witnessed a 400% year-on-year rise in the use of Stop and Search.

- In England, the total number of stops and searches in the year ending March 2013 decreased by 15% on the previous year. 36% of all stops and searches were in the Metropolitan Police area.

- In 2013, a NYC federal judge ruled that the use of the Stop, Question and Frisk policy violated New Yorkers' constitutional rights. Since this date considerably fewer people in NYC have been stopped and searched.

- In Europe, the use of non-statutory Stop and Search may be incompatible with Articles 5, 8 and 14 of the Human Rights Act 1998 in relation to the right to liberty, privacy and non-discrimination respectively.

- Stop and Search rates in Scotland are greatest amongst younger people. However, detection rates tend to be lower among younger age groups (those under the age of 20) due to the large number of searches carried out on young people. In 2010, approximately 500 children aged 10 years and under were stopped and searched by the police.

- In 2013, the Equality and Human Rights Commission (EHRC) said in some parts of England black people were 29 times more likely to be stopped and searched.

- Police Scotland believes that the operational use of Stop and Search powers is responsible for the fall in crime, especially knife crime. It acts as a major deterrent. A police spokesperson stated: 'Through intelligence Police Scotland aims to ensure we can bring an improvement to a community affected by crime and keep people safe.'

- Since Stop, Question and Frisk was introduced in NYC only around 6% of those stopped and frisked were subsequently arrested. More of those stopped and frisked were black and Hispanic.

- In the UK, Stop and Search aimed at deterring people from offending may damage people's trust and confidence in the police, and undermine public support for policing. A Liberal Democrat spokesperson asked: "Is it simply casting the net wide in hope of an eventual catch the best use of police time or the best deal for protecting civil liberties?"

- Of the 612,110 stops and searches by police officers in the Strathclyde area in 2012/13, 55.2% were carried out on the 16 to 29 age group, 83.8% were male and 97.1% white. Overall 12.6% were carried out on youths aged 15 and under. The black and minority ethnic population of the Strathclyde Police area in the 2011 census was recorded at 2.45% of the total population.

MARKS

Section 2 Question 1 (continued)

SOURCE B

Stop and Search per 10,000 people, England, Scotland and New York City between April 2013 and December 2013

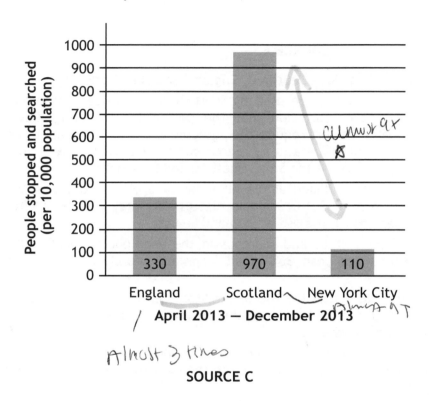

Almost 9x ∅

Almost 3 times

April 2013 – December 2013   Almost 9 T

SOURCE C

Scotland: Search powers by age group (%) 2012

Group	Non-statutory	Statutory	Total
0–14	83	17	32,522
15–20	78	22	186,674
21–25	70	30	68,750
26–30	65	35	45,110
31–35	65	35	33,164
36 +	68	32	64,867
Total	73	27	431,087

Attempt the following question, using **only** the information in Sources A, B and C opposite and above.

What **conclusions** can be drawn about the police and their use of Stop and Search?
You must draw conclusions about:

- the extent to which Stop and Search is used in different parts of the world
- the use of Stop and Search on different groups

You must give an **overall conclusion** on the use of Stop and Search.

8

Section 2 (continued)

MARKS

Attempt **EITHER** Question 2(a) **OR** 2(b) **OR** 2(c) **OR** 2(d)

Question 2

Part A: Social inequality in the United Kingdom

Answers may refer to Scotland or the United Kingdom or both.

(a) Analyse different views as to the main causes of social inequality in society.   **12**

OR

(b) Analyse different government policies in tackling inequalities in wealth.   **12**

Part B: Crime and the law in the United Kingdom

Answers may refer to Scotland or the United Kingdom or both.

(c) Analyse the different policies of the police in reducing crime.   **12**

OR

(d) Analyse whether criminal behaviour is caused by social factors.   **12**

SECTION 3 — INTERNATIONAL ISSUES — 20 marks

Attempt Question 1 and **EITHER** Question 2(a) **OR** 2(b) **OR** 2(c) **OR** 2(d)

Question 1

Study Sources A, B and C then answer the question that follows.

SOURCE A

US Foreign Policy in Obama's Presidency
On becoming President in November 2008, Barack Obama stated, "We will kill Bin Laden. We will crush al-Qaeda. That has to be our biggest national security priority." In 2009, a majority of the US public registered approval of Obama's foreign policy, far ahead of the figure achieved by recent US presidents. However, with the early failure to locate and capture Bin Laden, the American public became less supportive of Obama's foreign policy.
In May 2011, the US achieved its core aim of eliminating Bin Laden in his secret stronghold in Pakistan and US drone attacks (target bombings) have removed a further 30 top leaders of al-Qaeda. President Obama claimed recently that America had achieved its central goal: to dismantle al-Qaeda and prevent Afghanistan from being used as a future launch pad for attacks against America.
Obama, in his second term of office (re-elected 2012), continued to experience significant foreign policies challenges. For example, some political commentators have described American involvement in Libya as a failure. The USA and its European partners used air power to break Gadafi's army and rebels executed the long-time dictator. However, it is argued that US involvement in air strikes led to extremist groups in Libya looting huge stockpiles of weapons which were used to start conflict in neighbouring states such as Syria. On the anniversary of 9/11 in September 2012, a terrorist killed the US Ambassador and three of his colleagues in the American compound in Benghazi, Libya, which shocked and dismayed the US public.
In Syria, the US and its allies have supported the anti-government rebels fighting against the Syrian President Bashar al-Assad. However, a new fundamentalist group responsible for many of the attacks in Iraq and Syria, the Islamic State of Iraq and Syria (ISIS or Islamic State) is regarded as a major security threat to the area and the US. ISIS now controls large parts of Syria and northern Iraq. Obama openly admitted in summer 2014 that the US didn't as yet have a strategy for the fight against Islamic State. As a result, Obama's foreign policy approval in October 2014 fell to an all-time low. However, Obama's decision to engage in US-led coalition air strikes against Islamic State in Iraq and Syria has been welcomed by the American public — only 44 % disapproved.
Finally, on a brighter note, President Obama was able to announce that all US combat operations in Afghanistan would end in December 2014 with less than 10,000 US personnel remaining to support the Afghan government.
Adapted from various newspapers

MARKS

Section 3 (continued)

SOURCE B

Obama's Presidential Approval Ratings, 2009–2014 — Public Opinion Surveys (%)

Obama's Popularity
Job approval ratings, smoothed

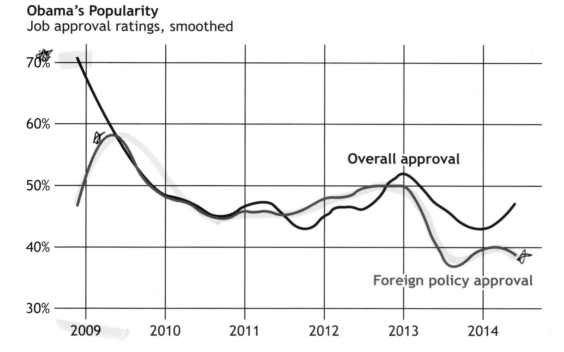

Source using polling data gathered by Huffpollster, a respected US polling agency

Use **only** the information in Source A and Source B to answer the following question.

To what extent is it accurate to state that President Obama's foreign policy is popular with the US public?

8

accurate

inaccurate

MARKS

Section 3 (continued)

Attempt **EITHER** Question 2(a) **OR** 2(b) **OR** 2(c) **OR** 2(d)

Question 2

Part A: World powers

(a)

A world power may claim that its political system is democratic.

Evaluate whether the political system of a world power you have studied is democratic.

12

OR

(b)

One aim of a world power is to tackle social and economic issues.

Evaluate the effectiveness of a world power you have studied in tackling social and economic issues.

12

OR

Part B: World issues

(c)

International organisations attempt to resolve world issues.

Evaluate the success of international organisations in resolving a world issue you have studied.

12

OR

(d)

World issues are caused by a mixture of political and/or socio-economic problems.

Evaluate the extent to which a world issue you have studied has been caused only by political problems.

12

[END OF MODEL PAPER 3]

SQA AND HODDER GIBSON HIGHER FOR CfE MODERN STUDIES 2014

General Marking Principles for Higher Modern Studies

Marking principles for each question type

For each of the question types the following provides an overview of marking principles.

The types of questions used in this paper are:
- Discuss ... [20 mark extended response]
- To what extent ... [20 mark extended response]
- Evaluate ... [12 mark extended response]
- Analyse ... [12 mark extended response]
- To what extent is it accurate to state that ... [information-handling question — 8 marks]
- What conclusions can be drawn ... [information-handling question — 8 marks]

Extended response (12 or 20 marks)

For 12 mark responses, up to a maximum of 8 marks will be awarded for knowledge and understanding (description, explanation and exemplification). The remaining marks will be awarded for the demonstration of higher-order skills of analysis or evaluation. Where a candidate makes more analytical/evaluative points than are required to gain the maximum allocation of 4 marks, these can be credited as knowledge and understanding marks provided they meet the criteria for this.

For 20 mark responses, up to 8 marks will be awarded for knowledge and understanding (description, explanation and exemplification). The remaining marks will be awarded for the demonstration of higher-order skills of analysis and evaluation and structured argument. Where a candidate makes more analytical/evaluative points than are required to gain the maximum allocation of marks, these can be credited as knowledge and understanding marks provided they meet the criteria for this.

In the *Democracy in Scotland and the United Kingdom* and the *Social Issues in the United Kingdom* sections, candidates should be credited for responses which refer to Scotland only, to the United Kingdom only, or to both Scotland and the United Kingdom in their responses.

Analyse questions
- Candidates will identify parts of an issue, the relationship between these parts and their relationships with the whole; draw out and relate implications.

Evaluate questions
- Candidates will make a judgement based on criteria; determine the value of something.

Discuss questions
- Candidates will communicate ideas and information on the issue in the statement. Candidates will be credited for analysing and evaluating different views of the statement/ viewpoint.

To what extent questions
- Candidates will analyse the issue in the question and come to a conclusion or conclusions which involve an evaluative judgement which is likely to be quantitative in nature.

Source-based questions that assess information-handling skills (8 marks)
- Questions will have at least two sources at an appropriate SCQF level.

- Award up to 3 marks for a single developed point depending on the use of the evidence in the sources and the quality of the analysis/evaluation.
- Credit candidates who synthesise information both within and between sources.
- For full marks candidates must refer to all sources in their answer.

'Objectivity' questions
- For full marks candidates must make an overall judgement as to the extent of the accuracy of the given statement. Maximum 6 marks if no overall judgement is made on extent of accuracy of the statement.
- Credit may be given up to 2 marks for answers which evaluate the usefulness or reliability of the source; however this is not required for full marks.

'Conclusions' questions
- For full marks candidates must make conclusions/ judgements based upon evidence relating to the specific prompts in the question.
- Candidates are also required to make an overall conclusion about the issue in the question.

Higher Modern Studies marking grid for 12 mark questions (KU = 8 marks; analysis/evaluation = 4 marks)

	1 mark	2 marks	3 marks	4 marks
Range of relevant knowledge Accurate, relevant, up-to-date	One relevant aspect of the issue given with some description	Two relevant aspects of the issue given with some description or one relevant aspect covered with detailed and accurate description	One relevant aspect of issue with detailed and accurate description **and** one relevant aspect with some description	At least two relevant aspects with detailed and accurate descriptions – these should include the key aspects of the issue
Quality of explanation/ exemplification of knowledge Up to a maximum of 8 marks available for knowledge and understanding	Some explanation of one aspect of the issue **or** relevant exemplification	Some explanation of two relevant aspects of the issue **or** detailed explanation of one aspect of the question which may include relevant exemplification	Detailed explanation of one relevant aspect of the issue with relevant exemplification **and** some explanation of one aspect of the question	At least two aspects of the question, fully explained, which relate closely to the key aspects of the question **and** extended, relevant, accurate and up-to-date exemplification
Analysis/evaluation Comments that identify relationships/ implications/make judgements 4 marks*	One relevant and accurate analytical or evaluative comment	One relevant and accurate analytical or evaluative comment that is justified **or** exemplified **or** two different relevant and accurate analytical/ evaluative comments	One developed relevant and accurate analytical or evaluative comment that is justified **and** exemplified – this should relate closely to a key aspect of the question	One extended, accurate and justified analytical or evaluative comment of an insightful nature which relates closely to the key aspects of the question and is exemplified

*Where a candidate makes more analytical/evaluative points than are required to gain the maximum allocation of 4 marks, these can be credited as knowledge and understanding marks provided they meet the criteria for this.

Answers to 12 mark questions should demonstrate at least two relevant aspects of knowledge.

For full marks (12/12), a response must include a range of points, have detailed description/explanation, include a range of accurate exemplification and analysis or evaluation.

For full marks in the KU aspect of the question (8 marks), a response **must** include a range of points, have detailed explanation, and include accurate exemplification. Maximum of 6 marks available (from 8 for KU) if there is no accurate or relevant exemplification.

Higher Modern Studies marking grid for 20 mark questions (KU = 8 marks; analysis/evaluation = 12 marks)

	1 mark	2 marks	3 marks	4 marks	5–6 marks
Range of relevant knowledge Accurate, relevant, up-to-date	One relevant aspect of the issue given with some description	Two relevant aspects of the issue given with some description **or** one relevant aspect covered with detailed and accurate description	One relevant aspect of the issue with detailed and accurate description **and** one relevant aspect with some description	At least two relevant aspects with detailed and accurate descriptions – these should include the key aspects of the issue	
Quality of explanation/ exemplification of knowledge Up to a maximum of 8 marks available for knowledge and understanding	Some explanation of one aspect of the issue or relevant exemplification	Some explanation of two relevant aspects of the issue **or** detailed explanation of one aspect of the question which may include relevant exemplification	Detailed explanation of one relevant aspect of the issue with relevant exemplification **and** some explanation of one aspect of the question	At least two aspects of the question, fully explained, which relate closely to the key aspects of the question **and** extended, relevant, accurate and up-to-date exemplification	
Analysis Comments that identify relationships/implications, explore different views or establish consequences/ implications Up to 6 marks*	One relevant and accurate analytical comment	One relevant and accurate analytical comment that is justified **or** exemplified **or** two different relevant and accurate analytical comments	One developed relevant and accurate analytical comment that is justified **and** exemplified: this should relate closely to a key aspect of the question	One extended, accurate and justified analytical comment of an insightful nature which relates closely to the key aspects of the question and is exemplified	At least two developed relevant and accurate analytical comments that are justified **and** exemplified. These should relate closely to the question and may be linked for 6 marks
Structure Structure which develops a consistent and clear line of argument Up to 2 marks	Clear structure that addresses the issue identified in the question	Structure that clarifies the issue, presents evidence and develops a clear and consistent line of argument			
Conclusions Evaluative comments which make a judgement(s) and or reach a conclusion(s) which address the key issues in the question Up to 4 marks*	One conclusion that addresses a key issue in the question	One extended and balanced conclusion that addresses a key issue in the question **or** two conclusions that address key issues in the question	One extended and balanced conclusion that is justified and directly addresses the key issue(s) in the question **or** two balanced conclusions that address the key issues in the question, one of which is extended	One extended and balanced insightful conclusion that is justified and directly addresses the central aspects of the question **and** which considers a range of viewpoints	

*Where a candidate makes more analytical/evaluative points than are required to gain the maximum allocation of 4 marks, these can be credited as knowledge and understanding marks provided they meet the criteria for this.

Answers to 20 mark questions should demonstrate at least two relevant aspects of knowledge and provide detailed analysis and evaluation. For full marks in the KU aspect of the question (8/8), a response must include a range of points, have detailed explanation, and include a range of accurate exemplification.

Maximum of 6 marks available (from 8 for KU) if there is no exemplification.

For full marks (20/20), a response must be structured, include a range of points, have detailed explanation, include a range of accurate and relevant exemplification and contain extended analysis and evaluation.

Higher Modern Studies marking grid for 8 mark source-based (objectivity/conclusions) questions

	1 mark	2 marks	3 marks	4 marks	5 marks	6 marks
Use of sources of evidence Up to 6 marks available	One relevant piece of evidence relating to one aspect of the issue is used from one source	Two distinct pieces of evidence relating to one aspect of the issue are linked which may be from within a single source or between sources	Two distinct pieces of evidence relating to one aspect of the issue are synthesised which may be from within a single source or between sources and an evaluative commentary is given	In addition; a second aspect of the issue is addressed with reference to one relevant piece of evidence	In addition; a second aspect of the issue is addressed with reference to linked evidence	In addition; a second aspect of the issue is addressed with reference to synthesised evidence including an evaluative commentary
Objectivity Analysis of the accuracy/selectivity/objectivity of a given view against evidence is presented Up to 2 marks available	An objective assessment of a given view is stated, based on evidence presented from the sources	A detailed objective assessment of a given view is stated, based on evidence presented from the sources	1. For full marks candidates **must** refer to all sources in their answer. A maximum of **6 marks** if all sources are not used. 2. **Objectivity questions.** (i) Up to **6 marks** are available for the accurate evaluation of the given view using evidence. (ii) Candidates may also be credited up to **2 marks** on any comment/analysis of the origin and reliability of the sources. (iii) Up to **2 marks** are available for an overall judgement as to the extent of accuracy/objectivity of the view. 3. **Conclusions questions.** For **full marks** candidates must make evaluative comments/judgement(s)/draw a conclusion about each of the points given in the question. **2 further marks** are available for an overall summative conclusion.			
Conclusions Overall evaluative comment(s) derived from a judgement of the evidence presented Up to 2 marks available	Overall conclusion is clear and supported by evidence from the sources	Overall conclusion is insightful and supported by detailed evidence from the sources				

HIGHER FOR CfE MODERN STUDIES
SPECIMEN QUESTION PAPER

Section 1: Democracy in Scotland and the United Kingdom

Question	General marking principles	Max mark	Detailed Marking Instructions for this question
1.	The candidate is required to interpret/ evaluate up to three complex sources of information detecting and explaining the extent of objectivity. In order to achieve credit candidates must show evidence which supports the extent of accuracy in a given viewpoint. • Award up to **3 marks** for appropriate use of evidence depending on the quality of the explanation and the synthesis of the evidence for any one explanation of the extent of objectivity. • For **full marks** candidates must refer to all sources in their answer. • For **full marks** candidates must make an overall judgement as to the extent of the accuracy of the given statement. • Maximum of **6 marks** if no overall judgement made on extent of accuracy of the statement. • Candidates may be awarded up to a maximum of **2 marks** for incorporating an evaluation of the reliability of the sources in their explanations, although this is not mandatory.	8	*Candidates can be credited in a number of ways **up to a maximum of 8 marks.*** **Evidence that supports the view** *(… the televised debates had a significant impact on voting intentions)* • The televised debates allowed voters to visually connect with candidates. *(1 mark)* • Ipsos MORI poll revealed 60% of voters felt the debates would help them decide who to vote for. *Link to Source 2 — before first live debate 14% of voters indicated they would not vote for the main parties; following the leaders' initial performances this had decreased to 8% with the main parties receiving a boost in percentages of voters who would vote for them. (2 marks)* • Coverage of the leaders during the debates could alter how the media reports on each of the leaders and their parties. *(1 mark)* • Success of TV debates increased Nick Clegg's popularity as a potential leader. *Link to Source 2 — 21% of voters claimed they would vote Liberal Democrat which rose to 32% following his performance during the first debate. (2 marks)* • Following the debates, an independent polling organisation found over a million voters (4% of voters) altered the way they would vote. *Link to Source 2 — before the first debate Conservatives had a 5-point lead which disappeared following the leader's first performance. (2 marks)* • TV debates motivated people to vote who may not have voted previously, with 17% rise in young voters indicating they would turn out to vote in some areas. *(1 mark)* **Evidence that does not support the view** *(…the televised debates had a significant impact on voting intentions)* • Only 12% said the survey changed their minds about who to vote for. *Link to Source 2 — very little change in percentages for Labour and Conservatives of voters who claimed they would vote for them in a General Election. (2 marks)* • *Source 1 — Initial viewing figures of 61% declined across the three debates. (1 mark)* • *Source 2 — Labour and Conservative vote remained largely unchanged. (1 mark)* Candidates may also be credited up to **2 marks** on any comment/evaluation of the origin and reliability of the sources. • Source A – "Various" sources — extent of adaptation not known. Source therefore not wholly reliable • Comment on reliability of statistics from Ipsos MORI (both sources) • Reliability of statistics from British Election Study 2010 — well-respected organisation

Question		General marking principles	Max mark	Detailed Marking Instructions for this question
1.		(continued)		• Independent company survey — no reference to size of sample for survey, limited information on connection of company to TV debates; however, independent therefore may be less likely to be biased • Source B — full reference, including date; widely respected polling organisation — more reliable. For full marks, candidates **must** make an overall judgement as to the extent of the accuracy of the given statement. Overall, the evidence **does not** support view as: • *Source 1 — Liberal Democrats came third with only 23% of the vote (up only 1% from 2005) despite appearing to do best in the debates.* • *Source 2 — actual election results very close to statistics in first pie chart taken before televised debates.*
2.	(a)	Evaluation involves making a judgement(s) based on criteria, drawing conclusions on the extent to which a view is supported by the evidence; counter-arguments including possible alternative interpretations; the overall impact/significance of the factors when taken together; the relative importance of factors in relation to the context. Credit responses that make reference to: • the main features of an electoral system • an evaluation of the success of the electoral system in providing for fair representation Up to **8 marks** for KU (description, explanation and exemplification) and up to **4 marks** for evaluative comments. Award up to **6 marks** per point. Candidates should be credited up to **full marks** if they answer within a Scottish context only, a UK context only or refer to both Scotland and the UK. Where a candidate makes more evaluative points than are required to gain the maximum allocation of 4 marks, these can be credited as knowledge and understanding marks provided they meet the criteria for this.	12	*Candidates can be credited in a number of ways **up to a maximum of 12 marks.*** **Credit reference to aspects of the following:** ***Additional Member System:*** • more opportunity to choose female or ethnic-minority candidates to increase representation • degree of proportionality allows for a wider range of parties to be featured in the Scottish Parliament which will benefit decision-making • number of votes gives voters a range of representatives from different parties with whom to discuss issues • increased accountability of representatives to voters • greater proportion of voters likely to get policy implemented that they voted for ***Balanced by:*** • impact of minority/majority government • impact of a coalition government, not directly voted for by voters • could be confusing for voters which may lead to a lower than normal turnout ***First Past the Post:*** • easy to understand and use in practice which could encourage turnout • direct link between MP and voters which increases accountability • usually produces a majority government which is able to drive through legislation in the interest of voters ***Balanced by:*** • tends to produce a two-party system: parliament has been dominated by two main parties in the post-war era — Labour and Conservative • impact of safe/marginal seats • no proportionality between votes and seats in some instances • government is often formed which is not reflective of voter choice • outdated electoral system as some parts of UK now have their own parliament as a result of devolution • it encourages tactical voting, as voters vote not for the candidate they most prefer, but against the candidate they most dislike *Any other valid point that meets the criteria described in the general marking principles for this type of question.*

Question		General marking principles	Max mark	Detailed Marking Instructions for this question
2.	(a)	(continued)		**Possible approaches to answering the question:** *Within the UK, a number of electoral systems are used to elect representatives to different parliaments. The Scottish Parliament uses the Additional Member System (AMS) to elect 129 MSPs and the UK Parliament uses First Past the Post (FPTP) to elect 650 MPs. (**1 mark KU**) The system used to elect the Scottish Parliament is said to provide better representation as voters get two votes whereas under FPTP they receive only one. (**1 mark evaluative comment**)* **(2 marks, one relevant point with limited description plus an evaluative comment)**

*It could be said that AMS provides better representation as voters have two votes which allows for wider choice. (**1 mark KU**) Voters have one vote for a constituency MSP and one vote for a regional list MSP which could lead to a higher turnout if voters know their second vote helps elect a regional MSP from the party they support. (**1 mark evaluative comment**) Under FPTP, voters have only one choice for a constituency MP. This has led to the claim that many votes are 'wasted' because with FPTP, only votes to the winning candidate count. Second-placed candidates get nothing. (**1 mark evaluative comment**)*

(3 marks, one relevant point with a developed explanation plus evaluative comment)

*Systems of proportional representation are said to be fairer and provide for better representation amongst voters and the type of government which they result in. Since devolution, Scotland has used AMS to elect the 129 MSPs, a mixture of FPTP to elect constituency MSPs and regional list to elect 'top up' MSPs. (**1 mark KU**) The fact that voters have more choice and can choose between candidates both within and between parties reduces the need for tactical voting and provides for better representation. (**1 mark evaluative comment**) It could be said that FPTP which is used to elect the 650 MPs to Westminster most often produces a clear result as voters have one clear vote for the candidate of their choice; however on occasion this has led to governments being formed with less than half the votes which is not representative of voter choice. (**1 mark KU, 1 mark evaluative comment**) In 2010, the Conservatives gained 36.1% of the vote, failing to reach the 326 majority needed to form a government, resulting in a coalition with the Liberal Democrats who achieved 23% of the vote. Many would argue this outcome is not reflective of their votes. (**1 mark KU, 1 mark evaluative comment**)*

(6 marks, one relevant point with a fully developed explanation and a range of accurate, up-to-date exemplification plus relevant extended, evaluative comment)

Question		General marking principles	Max mark	Detailed Marking Instructions for this question
2.	(a)	(continued)		*AMS is the system used to elect the Scottish Parliament. AMS is a form of proportional representation which is said to be fairer as it allows for wider representation compared to FPTP where the candidate with the most votes wins a seat in parliament and the party with the most MPs therefore becomes the government.* **(1 mark KU)** *Under AMS there is more often wider representation as it allows smaller political parties such as the Liberal Democrats and Green Party to gain representation.* **(1 mark KU)** *Under FPTP it tends to be the larger parties of Labour and Conservative which dominate government and which are more likely to hold an overall majority.* **(1 mark analysis)** **(3 marks, two relevant points made with some explanation, a relevant example and limited evaluative comment)** *FPTP is used to elect MPs to the UK Parliament and the party with the most MPs forms the UK government. In a constituency the person with the most votes wins but the winner does not need the majority of the vote. This is also true of the government.* **(1 mark KU)** *Since opening, the Scottish Parliament has used a form of proportional representation to elect MSPs called AMS. AMS is more proportional and means voters are more likely to get a candidate who they feel best represents them as the votes are distributed proportionally.* **(1 mark KU)** *AMS has been better for smaller parties such as the Liberal Democrats who do better under AMS than they would under FPTP.* **(1 mark KU)** *However, AMS more often leads to coalition politics which could affect decision-making. FPTP is more likely to produce a single party with a majority.* **(1 mark evaluative comment)** **(4 marks, two relevant points, a relevant example plus a limited evaluative comment)** *Overall, it could be argued that AMS does provide fair representation as more often than not there are representatives from a range of political parties in the Scottish Parliament and, apart from the election in 2011, different parties have had to work together to run the country and make laws.* **(1 mark analysis)** **(1 mark, overall evaluative comment that addresses the question)**
	(b)	Evaluation involves making a judgement based on criteria, drawing conclusions on the extent to which a view is supported by the evidence; counter-arguments including possible alternative interpretations; the overall impact/significance of the factors when taken together; the relative importance of factors in relation to the context.	12	*Candidates can be credited in a number of ways **up to a maximum of 12 marks**.* **Credit reference to aspects of the following (Scottish dimension):** • work of committees • questions to ministers • voting • Decision Time • debates and motions • impact of a majority/minority government • role and power of the whips • patronage power of the First Minister *Any other valid point that meets the criteria described in the general marking principles for this type of question.*

Question		General marking principles	Max mark	Detailed Marking Instructions for this question
2.	(b)	**(continued)** Credit responses that make reference to: • opportunities for parliamentary representatives to hold government to account • an evaluation of the effectiveness of parliamentary representatives in holding government to account Up to **8 marks** for KU (description, explanation and exemplification) and up to **4 marks** for evaluative comments. Award up to **6 marks** per point. Candidates should be credited up to **full marks** if they answer within a Scottish context only, a UK context only or refer to both Scotland and the UK. Where a candidate makes more evaluative points than are required to gain the maximum allocation of 4 marks, these can be credited as knowledge and understanding marks provided they meet the criteria for this.		**Possible approaches to answering the question (Scottish dimension):** *There are many ways in which MSPs can hold the Scottish government to account such as asking a question at First Minister's Question Time (FMQT) which takes place every Thursday. During FMQT MSPs have the opportunity to ask questions of the First Minister in the debating chamber. (1 mark)* **(1 mark, one relevant point made with an explanation)** *MSPs have a number of days in which they are able to hold the Scottish government to account. MSPs are able to submit a question to the presiding officer who will select six questions each week to be asked at FMQT which is every Thursday, lasting 30 minutes. (1 mark KU) FMQT allows individual MSPs the opportunity to answer subject-specific questions and general questions. In November 2012, First Minister Alex Salmond was asked about his figures for further education funding and was forced to apologise over misleading parliament with inaccurate information. (1 mark KU) Although not all questions are able to be asked, some MSPs may receive a written answer to their question instead. (1 mark evaluative comment)* **(3 marks, one relevant point with a fully developed explanation and accurate, up-to-date and relevant exemplification plus limited evaluative comment)** *One of the founding key principles of the Scottish Parliament when it opened in 1999 was accountability. The Scottish Parliament has a number of procedures in place to ensure this principle is met including ministers and FMQT which allows MSPs to regularly hold government to account. (1 mark KU) The First Minister is required to answer questions for 30 minutes every Thursday. On a number of occasions MSPs have posed questions to Alex Salmond about his government's actions. Depending on whether it is a minority or majority government this will have varying success. (1 mark evaluative comment) The SNP currently has a majority government which puts opposition at a disadvantage. However there are occasions where FMQT has proved effective. In November 2012, Alex Salmond was forced to apologise to MSPs for misleading them with claims that an independent Scotland would have automatic claims to EU membership following reports the SNP had sought legal advice which later proved to be inaccurate. (1 mark KU, 1 mark evaluative comment)* **(4 marks, one relevant point with a fully developed explanation and a range of accurate, up-to-date exemplification plus extended, qualified, evaluative comment)** *MSPs can influence the Scottish government and hold it to account in a number of ways. This can be done during FMQT, debates and discussions on proposed legislation such as the abolition of bridge tolls, and in committee work such as the Health Committee debating minimum alcohol pricing. MSPs can also vote on proposed laws. (2 marks KU) However, there must be a majority of MSPs in favour of a law before it can be passed. For example, all parties except Labour were in favour of the proposed Alcohol (Minimum Pricing) Bill. (1 mark evaluative comment)* **(3 marks, two relevant points with accurate and up-to-date exemplification plus relevant evaluative comment)**

Question		General marking principles	Max mark	Detailed Marking Instructions for this question
2.	(b)	(continued)		*Members of the Scottish Parliament can be very effective in holding the Scottish government to account. For example, there are a number of opportunities for MSPs to raise and debate issues, eg in parliamentary committees.* **(1 mark KU)** *Committees are made up of cross-party MSPs and they meet weekly or fortnightly to closely examine new laws or important Scottish issues.* **(1 mark KU)** *However, as the current Scottish government is a majority government, this means the SNP dominates most of the committees, such as the Health and Sports Committee, although this is chaired by a Labour MSP.* **(1 mark evaluative comment)** **(3 marks, one relevant point with a fully developed explanation and accurate, up-to-date exemplification plus evaluative comment)**
				In conclusion, MSPs can and do hold the Scottish government to account even if there is a majority government. The rules and procedures within the Scottish Parliament ensure all MSPs have the right to ask questions, be involved in committees and vote for and against legislation. Accountability is a key feature of the way in which the Scottish Parliament operates. **(2 marks, overall detailed evaluative comment that addresses the question)**
				Credit reference to aspects of the following (UK dimension): • debates • ministerial Question Time/Prime Minister's Question Time • voting • work of committees • impact of government majority/coalition • whip system • delaying power of House of Lords • motions of confidence
				Any other valid point that meets the criteria described in the general marking principles for this type of question.
				Possible approaches to answering the question (UK dimension): *There are many ways in which MPs in Parliament can hold the government to account. One way MPs can influence government is through the work of committees. There are a number of committees which meet in Parliament weekly to look at and discuss policies from each of the different departments, eg Health, Education, Transport and Environment.* **(1 mark KU)** **(1 mark, one relevant point explained)**
				There are numerous ways in which Members of Parliament can hold the government to account. One of the most effective ways is select committees. One role of a select committee is to scrutinise the work of government departments. **(1 mark KU)** *For example, the Health Committee recently met to discuss the role of the NHS at local level.* **(1 mark KU)** *Committees include a number of MPs from different political parties and they can be very effective in holding government to account. For example, Chancellor George Osborne was questioned by the Treasury Committee in 2011 over claims the 'windfall tax' could damage investment by the oil industry.* **(1 mark evaluative comment)** **(3 marks, one relevant point explained, with an example and an evaluative comment)**

Question		General marking principles	Max mark	Detailed Marking Instructions for this question
2.	(b)	(continued)		*Much of the work in the House of Commons and the House of Lords in holding the government to account is done through the work of committees. As a cross-party body, they have a minimum of 11 members whose job it is to examine issues in detail, including spending, government policy and proposed legislation. There are currently 19 committees in Westminster which gather evidence and make recommendations to the House of Commons based on their findings. **(2 marks KU)** However, government is under no obligation to act upon recommendations made and may reject them after a period of 60 days. It could be argued the work of committees is limited in holding government to account. **(1 mark evaluative comment)** Since 2010, however, the work of select committees has been strengthened by changes which now allow backbencher MPs to decide who represents the party and committee chairs are elected by secret ballot, which is arguably fairer than appointing committee members who are party loyalists. **(1 mark evaluative comment)** In January 2013, the Liaison Committee published a report re-examining the relationship between Parliament and government in light of the rising profile committees have played during investigations into claims of phone hacking, suggesting a 'growing role' for the committees. However this proposal was not accepted by government, highlighting that their work in holding the government to account is often limited. **(1 mark KU, 1 mark evaluative comment)*** **(6 marks, one relevant point with a fully developed explanation and a range of accurate and up-to-date exemplification plus relevant extended, qualified, evaluative comment)** *MPs have the right to question ministers (Question Time) and the Prime Minister (PMQT) and government ministers in both the Commons and the Lords. On a Wednesday when the Commons is sitting the PM will spend half an hour answering questions. **(1 mark KU)** However, there is never enough time to allow all MPs to ask questions with many critics claiming the PMQT is stage-managed and of little use in holding the government to account. **(1 mark evaluative comment)*** **(2 marks, one relevant point plus an evaluative comment)** *There are occasions when backbench MPs can have great influence on the decision-making in central government. For example, it is Parliament and not the government of the day that makes the decisions and the laws so a majority of all MPs must vote in favour before a decision is made. **(1 mark KU)** For example, MPs voted against UK military intervention in Syria and David Cameron had to accept the decision of Parliament. **(1 mark KU)** However, through the use of the party whip system, MPs are pressurised to vote according to the party's decision. The use of the party whip system, especially in a majority government, means there can be less of an effective check on the government. **(1 mark evaluative comment)*** **(3 marks, one relevant point, one example and one evaluative comment)** *To finish, the UK government is effectively held to account especially through the use of committees which have real power. However, asking questions and voting are less effective as a way of holding government to account as a result of time and the whip system. **(1 mark overall evaluative comment)*** **(1 mark overall evaluative comment that addresses the question)**

Section 2: Social Issues in the United Kingdom

Question	General marking principles	Max mark	Detailed Marking Instructions for this question
1.	The candidate is required to interpret/ evaluate up to three complex sources in order to reach conclusions. In order to achieve credit candidates must show evidence which explains the conclusions reached. • Award up to **3 marks** for appropriate use of evidence depending on the quality of the explanation and the synthesis of the evidence to reach any one conclusion. • For **full marks** candidates must refer to all sources in their answer. • For **full marks** candidates must reach conclusions about each of the points given and make an overall conclusion on the issue.	8	*Links between social exclusion and health:* • *Health is poorer in people who are socially excluded. People who are socially excluded usually have higher death and illness rates (Source 1). **(1 mark)*** • *Health is poorer in people who are socially excluded. People who are socially excluded usually have higher death and illness rates. (Source 1) This is backed up in Source 3 where Glasgow has 22% of people with long-standing illness which is the highest of the four local authority areas. **(2 marks)*** • *Source 1 states the factors causing social exclusion are inter-related. Source 3 shows that the poorest local authorities — such as Dundee and Glasgow which have the highest unemployment rates (5.9% and 5.8% respectively) — have a range of poorer statistics such as higher long-standing illness rates (Glasgow 22% and Dundee 17%) and higher premature death rates — Dundee is 3rd and Glasgow highest (Source 2). **(3 marks)*** *Links between social exclusion and local authority area:* • *Glasgow and Dundee have the highest premature death rates (Source 2) and this is backed up by Source 3 which shows Dundee and Glasgow have the highest unemployment rates. **(1 mark)*** • *Source 1 states that social exclusion is not equally spread across Scotland. This would be backed up by Source 3 which shows that Dundee (5.8%) and Glasgow (45%) have a higher percentage of the national share of the poorest parts of the country. **(2 marks)*** • *Source 1 states that social exclusion is not equally spread across Scotland and that there is a difference between urban and rural areas. This would be backed up by Source 3 which shows that Dundee (5.8%) and Glasgow (45%) have a higher percentage of the national share of the poorest parts of the country. **(2 marks)** There is further evidence in Source 2 to back this point up as Glasgow and Dundee have by far the highest levels of premature deaths, whereas more rural places such as Scottish Borders and Aberdeenshire have much lower premature death rates.* *Possible overall conclusions:* • *Overall, the evidence from each of the Sources 1–3 does suggest that social exclusion has a big impact in Scotland as it would appear that the poorest areas do have worse health and poorer social and economic data. **(1 mark)*** • *Overall, the evidence does suggest from Sources 1–3 that the factors that lead to social exclusion are strongly linked so that where social exclusion is greatest, health will be poorest. It is also clear that some parts of Scotland suffer more from social exclusion and these are also the local authority areas with the poorest social and economic data. **(2 marks)***

Question		General marking principles	Max mark	Detailed Marking Instructions for this question

2.	(a)	An analysis mark should be awarded where a candidate uses their knowledge and understanding/a source to identify relevant components (eg of an idea, theory, argument, etc) and clearly show at least one of the following:
		
		• links between different components
		• links between component(s) and the whole
		• links between component(s) and related concepts
		• similarities and contradictions
		• consistency and inconsistency
		• different views/interpretations
		• possible consequences/implications
		• the relative importance of components
		• understanding of underlying order or structure
		
		Credit responses that make reference to:
		
		• government policies to tackle social inequalities
		• an analysis of policies with reference to a specific group
		
		Up to **8 marks** for KU (description, explanation and exemplification) and up to **4 marks** for analytical comments
		
		Award up to **6 marks** per point.
		
		Candidates may make reference to specific groups facing inequality on the basis of, for example:
		
		• gender
		• race
		• employment/unemployment
		• income/poverty
		• disability
		
		Candidates should be credited up to **full marks** if they answer within a Scottish context only, a UK context only or refer to both Scotland and the UK as appropriate.
		
		Where a candidate makes more analytical points than are required to gain the maximum allocation of 4 marks, these can be credited as knowledge and understanding marks provided they meet the criteria for this.
			12	**Credit reference to aspects of the following:**
				• details of the Equality Act 2012
				• government policies, impact of the national minimum wage on female pay rates
				• gender pay gap, glass ceiling, over-representation in low-paid jobs, ie '5 Cs' (catering, cleaning, caring, clerical and cashiering)
				• impact of austerity measures, government cuts on welfare
				• reference to Equality and Human Rights Commission (EHRC) reports, Sex and Power Report, Joseph Rowntree Foundation (JRF)
				• rise in number of female-owned small businesses
				• women more likely to suffer poverty
				• credit also accurate references to other groups, eg ethnic minorities, people with disabilities, etc, and government policies to tackle inequalities
				
				Any other valid point that meets the criteria described in the general marking principles for this type of question.
				
				Possible approaches to answering the question:
				Gender inequality exists in the UK. Men get paid more than women and women struggle to get the better-paid jobs. Government has introduced various policies to tackle these inequalities. These policies include the Equality Act 2010. **(2 marks KU)**
				
				                    (2 marks, accurate point plus an example)
				
				Gender inequality exists in the UK. Men's average earnings are higher (often around 15% and higher in best-paid employment) than women's and, for many types of jobs, women still experience a 'glass ceiling' that acts as a barrier to them obtaining the better-paid and more senior jobs, eg CEOs in big multinational companies. **(2 marks KU)** *Government has attempted to reduce some of these inequalities by introducing a variety of laws such as the Equality Act 2010. One part of the Equality Act is to ensure equal pay for equal work between men and women, although many groups such as Engender feel pay equality will take years to achieve.* **(2 marks analysis)**
				
				As well as tackling pay inequality, the Equality Act aims to get rid of gender discrimination. It is illegal to discriminate in employment on grounds of gender. **(1 mark KU)** *Nonetheless there have been several high-profile examples where women have won their cases on grounds of gender discrimination (eg in London City banking jobs).* **(1 mark KU)** *The reality is that many women feel the law is not strong enough and more needs to be done to end gender discrimination in employment. Recently one study claimed one in four women returning to work after maternity leave is the subject of discrimination.* **(2 marks analysis)**
				        (8 marks, two separate accurate points, with description, explanation and exemplification plus extended analytical comment)

Question	General marking principles	Max mark	Detailed Marking Instructions for this question

(b)	An analysis mark should be awarded where a candidate uses their knowledge and understanding/a source to identify relevant components (eg of an idea, theory, argument, etc) and clearly show at least one of the following:
	
	• links between different components
	• links between component(s) and the whole
	• links between component(s) and related concepts
	• similarities and contradictions
	• consistency and inconsistency
	• different views/interpretations
	• possible consequences/implications
	• the relative importance of components
	• understanding of underlying order or structure
	
	Credit responses that make reference to:
	
	• lifestyle choices linked to poor health
	• an analysis of the consequences of specific lifestyle choices relating to poor health
	
	Up to **8 marks** for KU (description, explanation and exemplification) and up to **4 marks** for analytical comments.
	
	Award up to **6 marks** per point.
	
	Candidates should be credited up to **full marks** if they answer within a Scottish context only, a UK context only or refer to both Scotland and the UK as appropriate.
	
	Where a candidate makes more analytical points than are required to gain the maximum allocation of 4 marks, these can be credited as knowledge and understanding marks provided they meet the criteria for this.
		12	**Credit reference to aspects of the following:**
			• Poor lifestyle choices include smoking, excess alcohol consumption, lack of exercise, a diet high in salt and fat, drug misuse, or other risk-taking activities
			• Failure to make best use of preventative care services
			• Reference to government policies or health initiatives where it is acknowledged that these are a response to poor lifestyle choices, eg minimum alcohol pricing
			• Reference to official reports, eg Equally Well 2008 (and Inequalities Task Force Report 2010)
			• Statistical examples that highlight poor health in Scotland or the UK
			
			Any other valid point that meets the criteria described in the general marking principles for this kind of question.
			
			Possible approaches to answering the question:
			Some people choose to drink too much alcohol. Scotland has a culture of binge drinking especially at the weekend which costs the country a great deal of money. (1 mark KU)
			                    (1 mark, accurate and relevant point)
			
			Poor diet is a problem in Scottish society. Many people choose to eat too much fatty food such as burgers and chips. Too many people are now overweight or obese. Health campaigns such as the 5-a-day campaign to encourage people to eat more fruit and vegetables are a response to too many people choosing to eat a poor diet. (2 marks KU)
			                    (2 marks, accurate point with an example)
			
			Despite years of anti-smoking health campaigns or the ban on smoking in public places, some individuals continue to choose to smoke cigarettes. (1 mark KU) Around 22% of adults smoked in Scotland in 2012. (1 mark KU) As a consequence of smoking an individual is more likely to suffer from respiratory illness or lung cancer. Evidence shows that there is a strong link between smoking and lung cancer deaths. Around 90% of all lung cancer deaths are linked to people who smoked before they died. (2 marks analysis)
			                    (4 marks, accurate point with explanation, exemplification and analysis)
			
			There are many lifestyle choices that can be made to improve health. For example, people can choose not to smoke, drink too much alcohol or eat too much fatty food. (1 mark KU) Statistics show that Scotland has too many people who make the wrong lifestyle choices, eg around one in five adults smoke. (1 mark KU) Choosing to take regular exercise is another important way that people can stay fit and healthy. Walking or cycling to school or work regularly has been proven to improve people's health. Unfortunately, not enough people in Scotland take regular exercise. Studies show that less than half the adult population takes an hour's exercise at least three times per week. (2 marks KU) In Scotland the government has tried to encourage people to take more exercise by building cycle paths or by having subsidised entry to swimming pools or sports centres for children or people on a low income. The Equally Well Report of 2008 recognised that there was a need to promote exercise if Scotland was to further reduce the 'Big Three Killers' of heart disease, cancer and stroke. (2 marks analysis)
			                    (6 marks, accurate developed point, with description, explanation, exemplification and extended analysis)

Question	General marking principles	Max mark	Detailed Marking Instructions for this question
(c)	where a candidate uses their knowledge and understanding/a source to identify relevant components (eg of an idea, theory, argument, etc) and clearly show at least one of the following: • links between different components • links between component(s) and the whole • links between component(s) and related concepts • similarities and contradictions • consistency and inconsistency • different views/interpretations • possible consequences/implications • the relative importance of components • understanding of underlying order or structure Credit responses that make reference to: • government policies to tackle crime • an analysis of policies Up to **8 marks** for KU (description, explanation and exemplification) and up to **4 marks** for analytical comments. An analysis mark should be awarded Award up to **6 marks** per point. Candidates should be credited up to **full marks** if they answer within a Scottish context only, a UK context only or refer to both Scotland and the UK as appropriate. Where a candidate makes more analytical points than are required to gain the maximum allocation of 4 marks, these can be credited as knowledge and understanding marks provided they meet the criteria for this.	12	**Credit reference to aspects of the following:** The Scottish government has introduced or extended a range of policies to reduce crime or improve crime prevention including: • policies to tackle antisocial behaviour • policies on counteracting the threat of terrorism • drugs — recovery and enforcement • new laws give greater protection to victims of forced marriage • tougher sanctions on crime linked to racial, religious or social prejudice • action on human trafficking • tough enforcement and prevention measures • protecting children from exploitation and dealing with extreme materials • policies on tackling prostitution and kerb-crawling offences • reducing re-offending • tackling serious organised crime in Scotland • reforming rape and sexual offences law • tackling misuse of firearms and air weapons in Scotland • youth justice measures — early intervention and tackling youth crime • introducing specialist drug courts • community payback orders • restriction of liberty orders Measures to implement some of the above were contained in the Criminal Justice and Licensing (Scotland) Act 2010. In England and Wales, the Home Office claims emphasis is moving towards local community-based approaches to reducing crime, including improving crime prevention: • creating community triggers to deal with persistent antisocial behaviour • using community safety partnerships, and police and crime commissioners, to work out local approaches to deal with issues, including antisocial behaviour, drug or alcohol misuse and re-offending • establishing the national referral mechanism (NRM) to make it easier for all the different agencies that could be involved in a trafficking case to co-operate, share information about potential victims and access advice, accommodation and support • setting up the National Crime Agency (NCA) which will be a new body of operational crime fighters • creating street-level crime maps to give the public up-to-date, accurate information on what is happening on their streets so they can challenge the police on performance • creating the child sex offender disclosure scheme, which allows anyone concerned about a child to find out if someone in their life has a record for child sexual offences • legislating against hate crime • using football banning orders to stop potential trouble-makers from travelling to football matches both at home and abroad • legislation to prohibit cash payments to buy scrap metal and reforming the regulation of the scrap metal industry to stop unscrupulous dealers buying stolen metal The Antisocial Behaviour, Crime and Policing Bill was announced in May 2013. It aims to tackle a number of types of crime including antisocial behaviour, illegal use of firearms and organised crime.

Question		General marking principles	Max mark	Detailed Marking Instructions for this question
2.	(c)	(continued)		References can be made to Scottish and/or UK-based crime reduction policies. *Any other valid point that meets the criteria described in the general marking principles for this kind of question.* **Possible approaches to answering the question:** *To try and reduce crime in Scotland the Scottish government has announced it will increase the mandatory sentence for carrying a knife from four to five years. The Scottish government hopes this will stop young people carrying knives. (1 mark KU)* <div align="right">**(1 mark, accurate and relevant point)**</div> *In Scotland there are many early intervention programmes that have been introduced to try and reduce crime. One early intervention programme is 'Kick It Kick Off' (KIKO). (1 mark KU) This programme uses football to try and steer young people, many who have had problems at school or with the police, away from trouble. (1 mark KU) KIKO has been widely praised for its success in keeping many young people off the streets and out of trouble. KIKO programmes run in many parts of Scotland. (1 mark analysis)* <div align="right">**(3 marks, one accurate point explained with an example and analysis)**</div> *The Criminal Justice and Licensing (Scotland) Act 2010 strengthened the law in terms of racial or religiously motivated crime. Now, where it has been proved that someone has committed an offence on grounds of race or religion (hate crimes), the courts must take this into account when handing out the sentence. This can lead to a longer custodial sentence or higher fine or a different type of punishment where appropriate. (3 marks KU) Although many people support tougher punishments for hate crimes, arguing this will make some people think twice before committing a crime, there are those who believe longer or tougher sentencing is the wrong approach. These people would argue that there is little evidence tougher sentencing for hate crimes works. (2 marks analysis)* <div align="right">**(5 marks, one accurate developed point, with exemplification and extended analysis)**</div>
	(d)	An analysis mark should be awarded where a candidate uses their knowledge and understanding/a source to identify relevant components (eg of an idea, theory, argument, etc) and clearly show at least one of the following: • links between different components • links between component(s) and the whole • links between component(s) and related concepts • similarities and contradictions • consistency and inconsistency • different views/interpretations • possible consequences/implications • the relative importance of components • understanding of underlying order or structure Credit responses that make reference to: • a range of different crimes • an analysis of the consequences of crime for victims	12	**Credit reference to aspects of the following:** • reference to official crime figures or the Scottish Crime and Justice Survey, etc • range of types of crimes, eg violent and non-violent, and the short- and long-term effects of crime — physical, emotional, financial, psychological, etc • credit reference to crime where everyone is a victim in the widest sense, eg higher home/car insurance payments or more expensive prices when shopping • credit also references to the criminal justice system where again everyone in society is a victim in the widest sense • credit case studies and examples with reference to different crimes *Any other valid point that meets the criteria described in the general marking principles for this kind of question.* **Possible approaches to answering the question:** *To assault another person is a crime. This may result in a serious injury which requires medical attention. (1 mark KU) Physically a person may be hurt after an attack but they may also be frightened. Some people do not go out as much if they have been the victim of an assault. (1 mark analysis)* <div align="right">**(2 marks, accurate point explained plus analysis)**</div>

Question	General marking principles	Max mark	Detailed Marking Instructions for this question
2. (d)	**(continued)** Up to **8 marks** for KU (description, explanation and exemplification) and up to **4 marks** for analytical comments. Award up to **6 marks** per point. Candidates should be credited up to **full marks** if they answer within a Scottish context only, a UK context only or refer to both Scotland and the UK as appropriate. Where a candidate makes more analytical points than are required to gain the maximum allocation of 4 marks, these can be credited as knowledge and understanding marks provided they meet the criteria for this.		*Someone who has their handbag stolen is the victim of a crime. The result may be that the person loses money, their mobile phone or other personal belongings. (1 mark KU) Theft or crimes of dishonesty were the most common type of crime in 2011–12 in Scotland, accounting for around half of all recorded crime. (1 mark KU) However, when someone has their handbag stolen they may also become the victim of other crimes such as identity fraud. In some cases, thieves will attempt to use credit cards to purchase goods on the internet, running up thousands of pounds of illegal purchases. Unfortunately, the victim, who has done no wrong, may find they have to spend weeks or even months sorting out their finances. (2 marks analysis)* **(4 marks, one accurate and exemplified point with 2 marks for more detailed analysis)** *Being a victim of burglary is a serious issue. Although burglaries as a type of crime are falling in Scotland, there are many consequences as a result of a burglary. (1 mark KU) The first consequence of a burglary is that people lose many of their household possessions such as laptops and jewellery, some of which may have personal value. Emotionally this can be very upsetting. (1 mark analysis) Another consequence of a burglary, this time financial, is that a person's house insurance may jump. (1 mark analysis) If a victim or the area a victim lives in suffers repeat burglaries then they may not be able to obtain affordable insurance, meaning if their house gets broken into again they may not be able to replace the goods they lose. (1 mark KU) There is also a cost to wider society from burglaries as the cost of insurance for the general population will rise. (1 mark analysis) Thanks to better police investigation techniques and improved house alarm and controlled entry systems, the number of burglaries is falling although it remains a more common type of non-violent crime. (1 mark KU)* **(6 marks, accurate developed point, with description, explanation, exemplification and extended analysis)**

Section 3: International Issues

Question	General marking principles	Max mark	Detailed Marking Instructions for this question
1. (a)	An analysis mark should be awarded where a candidate uses their knowledge and understanding/a source to identify relevant components (eg of an idea, theory, argument, etc) and clearly show at least one of the following: • links between different components • links between component(s) and the whole • links between component(s) and related concepts • similarities and contradictions • consistency and inconsistency • different views/interpretations • possible consequences/implications • the relative importance of components • understanding of underlying order or structure	20	**Credit reference to aspects of the following:** **The powers of the US president include:** • determine foreign policy and diplomacy • propose legislation • issue executive orders • submit the budget to Congress — but can refuse to release money for legislation that he/she disapproves of • adjourn/recall Congress at any time • make appointments • Commander in Chief of armed forces • negotiates treaties • veto **Limits on the US president by the Congress may include:** • may impeach the president (House of Representatives) • conducts the trial for impeachment (Senate) • 'filibuster' and delay legislation — this usually results in a forced compromise with the president • make it difficult/delay bills getting through Congress if there are divisions between Congress and the president or within their own party

Question	General marking principles	Max mark	Detailed Marking Instructions for this question
1. (a)	**(continued)** Evaluation involves making a judgement based on criteria, drawing conclusions on the extent to which a view is supported by the evidence; counter-arguments including possible alternative interpretations; the overall impact/significance of the factors when taken together; the relative importance of factors in relation to the context. Credit responses that make reference to: • the political system in the world power • analysis of the ways the system checks government • balanced overall evaluative comment on the effectiveness of the political system in providing a check on government • provide a clear, coherent line of argument Up to **8 marks** for KU (description, explanation and exemplification) and up to **12 marks** for analytical/evaluative comments. Award up to **6 marks** per point. Candidates may make reference to any member of the G20 group of countries, excluding the United Kingdom. Where a candidate makes more analytical/evaluative points than are required to gain the maximum allocation of 4 marks, these can be credited as knowledge and understanding marks provided they meet the criteria for this.		• Supreme Court recommendations must be approved by the Senate • many appointments subject to approval by US Senate • refuse to pass any laws during special sessions called by the president • Congress declares war and allocates money to fund it • Congress scrutinises any treaties and a 2/3 Senate majority is required to ratify them **Powers of the US Supreme Court which may include:** • declare executive orders unconstitutional (judicial review) Credit also: • powers of the states • role of the media • role of interest groups *Any other valid point that meets the criteria described in the general marking principles for this kind of question.* **Possible approaches to answering the question — World Power: China** • CPC is one-party state — no effective opposition • other political parties are not in opposition to CPC • treatment of political opponents • development of 'grassroots democracy' including town and village elections, 'independent candidates', 'focus groups', channels of communication, etc. • CPC controls the media • Hong Kong — 'One Country: Two Systems' — free media, opposition parties, etc, but half the HK government appointed by CPC *Any other valid point that meets the criteria described in the general marking principles for this kind of question.* **Possible approaches to answering the question — World Power: USA** *The president has the power to veto legislation. This means that even if a new law has been passed by Congress, the president can refuse to sign, sending the bill back to Congress unsigned. For example, President Bush vetoed a bill to allow stem cell research in 2007. (2 marks KU)* **(2 marks, accurate point with an example)** *The president has the power to veto legislation. This means that even if a new law has been passed by Congress, the president can refuse to sign, sending the bill back to Congress unsigned. For example, President Bush vetoed a bill to allow stem cell research in 2007. (2 marks KU) There are two types of presidential veto — the regular veto where during a session of Congress the president returns a bill unsigned, and the 'pocket veto'. If either type of veto happens legislation cannot proceed. This is one of the 'checks and balances' in the US political system. (2 marks analytical comment)* **(4 marks, accurate point with explanation, exemplification and analytical/evaluative comment)**

Question		General marking principles	Max mark	Detailed Marking Instructions for this question
1.	(a)	(continued)		*The president has the power to veto legislation. This means that even if a new law has been passed by Congress, the president can refuse to sign, sending the bill back to Congress unsigned. For example, President Bush vetoed a bill to allow stem cell research in 2007.* **(2 marks KU)** *There are two types of presidential veto — the regular veto where during a session of Congress the president returns a bill unsigned, and the 'pocket veto'. If either type of veto happens legislation cannot proceed. The pocket veto occurs when Congress is adjourned and the president refuses to sign and the bill fails. By 2012, President Obama had twice used the pocket veto. This is one of the 'checks and balances' in the US political system.* **(2 marks KU range of knowledge and 2 marks analytical comment).** *However, there are limits to the president's power to veto legislation. For example, if two-thirds of both Houses of Congress (Senate and Representatives) vote to override a presidential veto, the bill becomes law, eg the Medicare Bill was overridden by Congress in 2008. Then again, Congress can vote to override a presidential veto, causing the bill to become law without the president's approval, although this has rarely happened.* **(2 marks evaluative comment)** **(8 marks, range of knowledge, description/explanation, exemplification and extended analytical/evaluative comment)** *Overall, there are many checks and balances within the US system of government that provide for an effective check on the government. The president may have many important powers such as control of the armed forces but Congress and on occasion the Supreme Court can check these powers. There is also the separation of powers between state governments and the federal government. This too ensures that no one part of government can become too powerful. The US Constitution defines clearly those powers that are given to states such as issuing licences (driving, firearms, etc), those that are shared and those that are given to the federal government. Taken as a whole, the US political system is very effective in checking the different parts of government.* **(4 marks conclusions)** **(4 marks, balanced overall comment plus 2 marks for structure/line of argument)**
	(b)	An analysis mark should be awarded where a candidate uses their knowledge and understanding/a source to identify relevant components (eg of an idea, theory, argument, etc) and clearly show at least one of the following: • links between different components • links between component(s) and the whole • links between component(s) and related concepts • similarities and contradictions • consistency and inconsistency • different views/interpretations • possible consequences/implications • the relative importance of components • understanding of underlying order or structure	20	**Credit reference to aspects of the following:** **Possible approaches to answering the question — World Power: USA** • leading role as a permanent member of the UN Security Council • examples of US involvement in Afghanistan (ISAF) • leading role in NATO — examples of US involvement in Libya as part of Operation Unified Protector • possible future role of US in Syria • member of the G8 • largest economy in the world • role in Middle East • nuclear superpower • impact of emergence of China as superpower • withdrawal from Iraq/Afghanistan *Any other valid point that meets the criteria described in the general marking principles for this kind of question.*

Question		General marking principles	Max mark	Detailed Marking Instructions for this question
1.	(b)	Evaluation involves making a judgement based on criteria, drawing conclusions on the extent to which a view is supported by the evidence; counter-arguments including possible alternative interpretations; the overall impact/significance of the factors when taken together; the relative importance of factors in relation to the context. Credit responses that make reference to: • role/part played by world power in international relations • analysis of the importance of world power in international relations • balanced overall evaluative comment on the importance of the world power in international relations • provide a clear, coherent line of argument Up to **8 marks** for KU (description, explanation and exemplification) and up to **12 marks** for analytical/evaluative comments. Award up to **6 marks** per point. Candidates may make reference to any member of the G20 group of countries, excluding the United Kingdom. Where a candidate makes more analytical/evaluative points than are required to gain the maximum allocation of 4 marks, these can be credited as knowledge and understanding marks provided they meet the criteria for this.		**Possible approaches to answering the question — World Power: China** **Credit reference to aspects of the following:** • leading role as a permanent member of the UN Security Council • participates in UN peace-keeping operations • relationship with and future role in negotiations with North Korea • impact of US/China diplomatic relations • investment in African countries and elsewhere • growing importance of China in world economy (2nd to the USA and expected to pass) • member of the G20 • part of the G8's Outreach Five (O5) *Any other valid point that meets the criteria described in the general marking principles for this kind of question.* **Possible approaches to answering the question — World Power: USA** *The USA's role as a world power is very important. It was one of the original countries that set up NATO in 1949 and still remains its most influential member. More recently the USA has played the lead role in NATO's mission to Afghanistan (ISAF). (2 marks KU)* **(2 marks, accurate and exemplified but underdeveloped point)** *The USA's role as a world power is very important. It was one of the original countries that set up NATO in 1949 and still remains its most influential member. More recently the USA has played the lead role in NATO's mission to Afghanistan (ISAF). (2 marks KU) In terms of finance, troop and resource commitments to NATO, the USA provides far more than any other single member of the Alliance, making the US the most important member of NATO, so in one sense the US can be seen as the most important member of the world's most powerful alliance. (1 mark analysis)* **(3 marks, accurate point with explanation, exemplification and analytical comment)** *The USA's role as a world power is very important. It was one of the original countries that set up NATO in 1949 and remains its most influential member. More recently the USA has played the lead role in NATO's mission to Afghanistan (ISAF). (2 marks KU) In terms of finance, troop and resource commitments to NATO, the USA provides far more than any other single member of the Alliance, so in one sense the US can be seen as the most important member of the world's most powerful alliance. (1 mark analysis) However, in recent years the USA has called on the other members of NATO to pay a greater share of the organisation's costs. The USA has also withdrawn a great many troops and resources from Europe in the expectation that European NATO members will do more for their own defence. (1 mark analysis comment) Although the USA may dominate NATO in terms of its contribution, NATO's 28 members have equal standing, ie no one member country has more voting rights than the next and there must be agreement by all before action can be taken. This meant that for NATO to invade Afghanistan after 9/11, for example, all the members had to be in agreement. (2 marks analysis/evaluative comment)* **6 marks, accurate and developed point, exemplified with extended analytical/evaluative comment)**

Question		General marking principles	Max mark	Detailed Marking Instructions for this question
1.	(b)	**(continued)**		*Therefore, given the importance of the USA within NATO, the UN, and the global economy, it is clear the USA is, at present, the world's most important country. For example, the US is sometimes described as 'the leader of the free world'. However, China is closing the gap in terms of the importance of the US to the world economy, as are the rest of the BRIC countries. Further, China has entered the space race and is increasing its influence in Africa. Also, despite US/NATO military strength in Afghanistan, the Taliban has not been defeated. The USA may be the world's only 'superpower' but this does not mean it has the power to achieve everything it seeks. **(4 marks conclusion)*** ***(4 marks, balanced overall comment)***
	(c)	An analysis mark should be awarded where a candidate uses their knowledge and understanding/a source to identify relevant components (eg of an idea, theory, argument, etc) and clearly show at least one of the following: • links between different components • links between component(s) and the whole • links between component(s) and related concepts • similarities and contradictions • consistency and inconsistency • different views/interpretations • possible consequences/implications • the relative importance of components • understanding of underlying order or structure Evaluation involves making a judgement based on criteria, drawing conclusions on the extent to which a view is supported by the evidence; the relative importance of factors; counter-arguments including possible alternative interpretations; the overall impact/significance of the factors when taken together; the relative importance of factors in relation to the context. Credit responses that make reference to: • responses of international organisations to a significant world issue • analysis of the ways international organisations attempt to resolve a world issue • provide a clear, coherent line of argument Up to **8 marks** for KU (description, explanation and exemplification) and up to **12 marks** for analytical/evaluative comments. Award up to **6 marks** per point Candidates may make reference to any world issue the impact of which extends beyond the boundaries of any single country. This impact may be regional or global in scale.	20	**Credit reference to aspects of the following:** • world issue: international terrorism (UN/NATO) • world issue: developing world poverty (UN agencies/NGOs) • world issue: nuclear proliferation (UN) • world issue: global economic crisis (EU/World Bank/IMF) *Any other valid point that meets the criteria described in the general marking principles for this kind of question.* **Possible approaches to answering the question:** *The threat of the development of nuclear weapons by countries such as North Korea and Iran continues to be a major concern for the United Nations. As North Korea and Iran are not seen as stable democracies, it is a concern for the UN that either acquires nuclear capability. **(1 mark KU)*** ***(1 mark, accurate but underdeveloped point)*** *The threat of the development of nuclear weapons by countries such as North Korea and Iran continues to be a major concern for the United Nations. The Treaty on the Non-Proliferation of Nuclear Weapons (updated 1995) was signed by 190 countries including North Korea. As North Korea and Iran are not seen as stable democracies, it is a concern for the UN that either acquires nuclear capability. **(2 marks KU)** By way of response, the UN has imposed a variety of trade sanctions against North Korea and Iran. These sanctions aim to limit North Korea's ability to gain access to technology that would allow both countries to arm nuclear missiles. So far this policy seems to be partly working as it is claimed Iran has no nuclear weapons. **(2 marks analysis)*** ***(4 marks, accurate point with explanation, exemplification and analysis)***

Question		General marking principles	Max mark	Detailed Marking Instructions for this question
1.	**(c)**	**(continued)** Where a candidate makes more analytical/evaluative points than are required to gain the maximum allocation of 4 marks, these can be credited as knowledge and understanding marks provided they meet the criteria for this.		*The threat of the development of nuclear weapons by countries such as North Korea and Iran continues to be a major concern for the United Nations. The Treaty on the Non-Proliferation of Nuclear Weapons (updated 1995) was signed by 190 countries including North Korea. As North Korea and Iran are not seen as stable democracies, it is a concern for the UN that either acquires nuclear capability.* **(2 marks KU)** *By way of response, the UN has imposed a variety of trade sanctions against North Korea and Iran. These sanctions aim to limit North Korea's ability to gain access to technology that would allow both countries to arm nuclear missiles. So far this policy seems to be partly working as it is claimed Iran has no nuclear weapons.* **(2 marks analysis)** *Despite these UN sanctions, the North Koreans continue to test or threaten to test nuclear weapons, increasing international tension. Recently, the North Koreans have talked of re-starting their nuclear programme to create nuclear material that could be used in weapons. They have also threatened to take action against South Korea and the USA which runs the risk of starting a devastating war. UN Secretary-General Ban Ki-moon has intervened to ask all sides to step back and, because of the seriousness of the situation, to think carefully about what they say.* **(3 marks analytical/evaluative comment, 1 mark structure)** **(8 marks, structure, description/explanation, exemplification and extended analytical/evaluative comment)** *Taken together, it can be argued that the United Nations has only been partly successful in attempting to limit the spread of nuclear weapons. Although around 200 countries signed up to the Treaty on the Non-Proliferation of Nuclear Weapons, and most countries of the world do not wish to develop nuclear weapons or share nuclear technology (some have even ended their interest in nuclear technology), more countries have become nuclear states or are suspected of having the capability to build or launch a nuclear missile. Unfortunately, the reality is that if some countries retain nuclear weapons then there will be others who will also want them.* **(4 marks conclusion)** **(4 marks, balanced overall comment)**
	(d)	An analysis mark should be awarded where a candidate uses their knowledge and understanding/a source to identify relevant components (eg of an idea, theory, argument, etc) and clearly show at least one of the following: • links between different components • links between component(s) and the whole • links between component(s) and related concepts • similarities and contradictions • consistency and inconsistency • different views/interpretations • possible consequences/implications • the relative importance of components • understanding of underlying order or structure	20	**Credit reference to aspects of the following:** • war — Afghanistan, Libya, Syria • nuclear weapons — North Korea • borders — Middle East • economic difficulties — EU countries (Portugal, Ireland, Italy, Greece, Spain) • factors which limit development *Any other valid point that meets the criteria described in the general marking instructions for this kind of question.* **Possible approaches to answering the question:** **Factors which affect development:** *One international issue is the lack of development in many countries in Africa. The lack of healthcare and education are said to be two of the most important factors limiting development.* **(1 mark KU)** **(1 mark accurate but underdeveloped point)**

Question		General marking principles	Max mark	Detailed Marking Instructions for this question
1.	(d)	**(continued)** Evaluation involves making a judgement based on criteria, drawing conclusions on the extent to which a view is supported by the evidence; the relative importance of factors; counter-arguments including possible alternative interpretations; the overall impact/ significance of the factors when taken together; the relative importance of factors in relation to the context. Credit responses that make reference to: • explanation of the international issue • analysis of the impact of the issue in different countries • balanced overall evaluative comment on the extent to which an international issue has impacted on people in different countries • provide a clear, coherent line of argument Up to **8 marks** for KU (description, explanation and exemplification) and up to **12 marks** for analytical/ evaluative comments. Award up to **6 marks** per point. Candidates may make reference to any world issue the impact of which extends beyond the boundaries of any single country. This impact may be regional or global in scale. Where a candidate makes more analytical/evaluative points than are required to gain the allocation of 4 marks, these can be credited as knowledge and understanding marks provided they meet the criteria for this.		*One international issue is the lack of development in many countries in Africa. The lack of available and affordable healthcare and education are said to be two of the most important factors limiting development. (**1 mark KU**) For example, in Malawi life expectancy is low (54 years) and illiteracy rates are high (one in six people cannot read or write). (**1 mark KU**) However, in recent years many African countries have seen real improvements in standards of living, many experiencing faster economic growth than countries in Europe. (**1 mark analytical comment**) Free from civil war, the people of countries such as Mozambique and Angola have been able to invest in schools and medical clinics and have made progress in reducing illnesses such as HIV/AIDS or increasing the number of children in primary school. (**1 mark analysis, 1 mark KU**)* **(5 marks, accurate point with explanation, exemplification and extended analysis/evaluative comment)** *Overall, development in African countries has been mixed if, for example, measured against the UN's Millennium Development Goals. Countries that have experienced good government and have been free from war, such as Tanzania and Ghana, have made sustained progress. However, where the government has been accused of corruption (Nigeria) or where there has been conflict (Sudan), there has been much less progress. (**3 marks conclusion**)* **(3 marks, balanced overall comment)**

General Marking Principles Model Papers 1—3

Skills Question — Explaining selectivity/objectivity

The candidate is required to evaluate up to three complex sources detecting and explaining selectivity.

Candidates can be credited in a number of ways **up to a maximum of 8 marks.**

In order to achieve credit candidates must show evidence that supports the extent of accuracy of a given viewpoint.

- Award up to three marks for appropriate use of a source, depending on the quality of the explanation and the development of the evidence to support and/or not support a view.

- For full marks candidates **must** refer to all sources. A maximum of **four** marks if only one source used and a maximum of **six** marks if only two sources used.

- For full marks evidence **must** be cited that both supports and opposes the given view. Maximum of **six** out of eight if only one side given.

- For full marks candidates **must** make an overall judgement as to the extent of accuracy of the given statement. Maximum of **six** marks if no overall judgement made on the extent of the accuracy of the statement.

- Up to **two** marks also available for accurate comment/analysis of the origin and reliability of the sources.

Skills Question — Reaching conclusions

The candidate is required to interpret/evaluate up to three complex sources in order to reach conclusions.

In order to achieve credit candidates must show evidence that explains the conclusions reached.

- Award up to **three** marks for appropriate use of evidence depending on the conclusion.

- For full marks candidates **must** refer to all sources in their answer.

- For full marks candidates **must** reach a conclusion about each of the points given and make an overall conclusion on the issues.

Extended Response — Evaluate

Evaluation involves making a judgement based on criteria, drawing conclusions on the extent to which a view is supported by the evidence; counter-arguments including possible alternative interpretations; the overall impact/significance of the factors when taken together; the relative importance of factors in relation to the context.

Up to **8 marks** for KU (description, explanation and exemplification) and up to **4 marks** for evaluative comments.

Extended Response — Analyse — 12 marks

Analysis involves using knowledge and understanding to identify and link aspects of the following: relevant arguments, different viewpoint, statistical sources, theories and implications.

Up to **8 marks** for KU (description, explanation and exemplification) and up to **4 marks** for analysis and structured answers. Award up to 6 marks per point.

Extended Response — To what extent, Discuss — 20 marks

Analysis involves using knowledge and understanding to identify and link aspects of the following: relevant arguments, different viewpoint, statistical sources, theories and implications.

Evaluation involves making a judgement based on criteria, drawing conclusions on the extent to which a view is supported by the evidence; counter-arguments including possible alternative interpretations; the overall impact/significance of the factors when taken together; the relative importance of factors in relation to the context.

Up to **8 marks** for KU (description, explanation and exemplification) and up to **12 marks** for analysis and structured answers. Award up to 6 marks per point.

(See pages 53–56 for further details of general marking principles.)

HIGHER FOR CfE MODERN STUDIES
MODEL PAPER 1

Section 1 — Democracy in Scotland and UK

Question		Detailed marking principles	Max mark
1.		**What conclusions can be drawn** Credit reference to aspects of the following: **The success of UKIP** • *Source A: UKIP won the most votes and seats in the European Parliament. This is supported in Source B with UKIP winning 22 seats in England to Labour's 18 and receiving 27.5% of votes compared to Labour's 23.9%.* **(2 marks)** • *Source A: UKIP topped the poll in six of the nine English regions and in the South-East it doubled its MEPs to four.* **(1 mark)** • *Source B: Outside Scotland, UKIP almost doubled its MEPs rising from 12 to 23.* **(1 mark)** *UKIP also increased its votes (from 16.5% outside Scotland to 27.5%).* **(1 mark)** • *Source A: In Scotland and Wales, UKIP increased its share of the vote and gained its first ever Scottish MEP and retained their Welsh seat. Source C: In Scotland UKIP doubled its vote from 5.2% to 10.4%* **(2 marks)** **The success of other parties** • *Source A: For the Liberal Democrats it was a disastrous performance. Source B: The Liberal Democrats vote halved from 13.8 % to 6.9%* **(2 marks)** • *Source A: The Liberal Democrats performance was disastrous. Source B: Outside Scotland Lib Dems lost nine of their 10 MEPs. Source C: In Scotland they lost their only seat.* **(2 marks)** • *Source A: Labour came second after UKIP. Source B: Outside Scotland Labour returned 18 MEPs securing 25.4% of the vote.* **(2 marks)** • *Source C: In Scotland, the SNP did best having the largest number of votes (29%) and both Labour and SNP had two seats each.* **(2 marks)** **Possible overall conclusions:** • *Overall, the evidence from each of the Sources A–C suggests that UKIP was the most successful party as it won the most votes and seats in Great Britain and the Liberal Democrats were the least successful in Great Britain.* **(1 mark)** • *Overall, the evidence suggests from Sources A–C that the result of the 2014 European election 2014 in the UK was an outstanding success for UKIP. UKIP won the most votes and seats in Great Britain (outside Scotland) and also gained its first seat in Scotland. The Liberal Democrats were the least successful as they lost a significant number of votes and seats both within and outwith Scotland.* **(2 marks)** *Any other relevant point.*	8
2.	(a)	**Evaluate** **Credit responses that make reference to:** • Opportunities for parliamentary representatives to scrutinise government • An evaluation of the effectiveness of parliamentary representatives in scrutinising government **Credit reference to aspects of the following (Scottish dimension):** • Debates, questions to ministers, motions and voting • Role of committees • Role and influence of Whips • Patronage power of the First Minister • Impact of a majority/minority government *Any other valid point that meets the criteria described in the general marking principles for this type of question.* **Possible approaches to answering the question (Scottish dimension):** *There are many ways for opposition MSPs to scrutinise the Scottish Government. One important way is First Minister's Question Time (FMQT). This takes place every Thursday and this enables the leaders of the main opposition parties and other MSPs to ask questions of the First Minister on events that are important to the people of Scotland.* *(2 marks, one relevant point made with explanation)*	12

Question		Detailed marking principles	Max mark
2.	(a)	**(continued)**	

Holding the government to account is considered one of the key strengths of the Scottish Parliament. As such there are many ways in which MSPs can scrutinise the work of the Scottish Government. For example, MSPs can raise issues within the Chamber of the Scottish Parliament, initiate debates and propose courses of action by using motions. Using a motion, the proposer is given 7 minutes to introduce their motion and it is usually replied to by a Government Minister. This forces the Scottish Government to explain itself. Motions are then debated in the Chamber. At Decision Time MSPs vote on whether to agree or reject the motion.

(3 marks, broad point followed by extended development of a final point)

Committees play an important role in scrutinising the Scottish Government with all legislation being considered by a committee. Committees work more on cross-party lines and there tends to be agreement among MSPs from different parties when scrutinising or challenging the work of the Scottish Government. Chairs are sometimes chosen from opposition parties. Committees can conduct inquiries, take on fact finding visits and produce reports. They can put forward their own proposals for new legislation (known as Committee Bills). However, with the SNP now having a majority of MSPs, this enables the SNP to dominate committees and the opposition parties claim it is now more difficult to call the Scottish Government to account.

(4 marks, accurate point with developed explanation, exemplification and evaluative comment)

Question Time enables the leaders of the main opposition parties and other MSPs to ask questions of the First Minister. When time allows, MSPs can ask general questions of Cabinet Ministers — a recent example which received much media coverage was Police Scotland patrolling peaceful streets fully armed. This forced the Cabinet Secretary for Justice (Kenny MacAskill) to justify this new policy. MSPs were also very effective in forcing the government to reconsider its decision to scrap corroboration. However FMQT only lasts 30 minutes and Cabinet Ministers' questions only 20 minutes, so it can be argued that this short time available weakens scrutiny of the Scottish Government.

(4 marks, accurate point with developed explanation and with evaluative comment

In conclusion, despite a majority SNP government since 2011, MSPs can be effective in scrutinising all government action. All MSPs have the opportunity to challenge government actions, be active in committees and vote for and against legislation. However it is now more difficult to defeat government bills.

(2 marks, overall detailed evaluative comment that addresses the question)

Credit reference to aspects of the following (UK dimension):
- Debates, questions to ministers, motions and voting
- Role and powers of committees
- Role and influence of Whips
- Patronage power of the Prime Minister
- Impact of coalition government

Any other valid point that meets the criteria described in the general marking principles for this type of question.

Possible approaches (UK dimension):

One important way that MPs can scrutinise the government is through committees. These committees meet every week when parliament is in session and examine the actions of different government departments such as the Department for Work and Pensions.

(1 mark, one relevant point explained)

One of the most effective ways MPs can scrutinise government action is through the work of committees. Select committees examine the actions of government departments. The committees have the power to question ministers, call witnesses and review documents although they cannot force MPs or ministers to attend. Most MPs do attend, however, as refusal to attend or answer questions can damage a parliamentary representative's public profile. After an investigation, committees will produce a report which often gains public attention. For example, a select committee heavily criticised the government for selling off the Royal Mail for too low a figure, costing the taxpayers millions in lost revenue.

(4 marks, accurate point with explanation and analytical comment)

Question		Detailed marking principles	Max mark
2.	(a)	**(continued)** *The existence of a coalition government has increased MPs' ability to scrutinise and challenge government policies. This is because no one party has control of the House of Commons and there is a greater chance that policies proposed by the coalition (such as reform of the House of Lords which the Lib Dems support) may be challenged by MPs from their Conservative partners in the coalition. In 2012, the Conservative–Liberal Democrat Coalition Government, faced with a Conservative backbench revolt, dropped part of its plans to reform the House of Lords. Another example was in 2013 when MPs voted against UK military action in Syria in response to Syria's use of chemical weapons on its own people.* *(4 marks, accurate point with developed explanation and extended up-to-date exemplification plus evaluative comment)* *One of the most effective ways MPs can scrutinise government action is through the work of select committees which look closely at the work of government departments (Treasury Select Committee) or issues affecting the country (the economy). In parliament, select committees gather evidence and make recommendations to the House of Commons or the House of Lords. However, the select committees' reports and recommendations can be ignored by the government.* *Membership of select committees (or general committees which look at legislation) reflects party strength so they may well be dominated by government MPs. This strengthens one view that committees are weak in scrutinising the government. However some recent reforms have, it is claimed, made committees more effective. The chairperson is now elected on a free and secret ballot of all MPs. Also, backbench MPs — not party whips — decide who should represent their party on each committee. Arguably, this improves the effectiveness of committees.* *(5 marks, accurate point with fully developed explanation and up-to-date exemplification plus evaluative comment)* *In conclusion, the coalition government's majority in parliament limits, to an extent, effective scrutiny by parliamentary representatives. However, recent reforms to the committee system, it has been argued, will improve the effectiveness of parliament in scrutinising the government.* *(2 marks, overall evaluative comment that addresses the question)*	
	(b)	**Evaluate** **Credit responses that make reference to:** • Factors which influence voting behaviour • Evaluation of different factors which influence voting behaviour **Credit reference to aspects of the following (Scottish and/or UK dimension):** • Importance of social class and recent trends. The period between 1979 and today is described as one of declining party identification and partisan de-alignment. Many traditional Labour voters switched to SNP in the 2011 Scottish Parliament elections. • Other long-term factors such as age, ethnicity and gender. Clear link between age and party support; the young more likely to vote Labour and older voters to choose the Conservatives. Ethnic minority voters are more likely to vote Labour. However, ethnicity can be affected by short-term issues such as Labour Government's support for Iraq war. • Regional variations. North-South divide is evident with anti-Conservative support highest in Scotland, Wales and the north of England. The Conservatives' strongest support is in southern England and English suburbs and rural areas. Link here to social class. • Short-term influences such as party policies, image of party leaders and issue voting. Leadership of Gordon Brown became a key issue in 2010 General Election. • Role of media in influencing voters including newspapers, television, radio, etc. Also, growing influence of new media (internet) and social media. However the success of Nick Clegg in the 2010 party leaders' debate did not translate into more votes for the Liberal Democrats. *Any other valid point that meets the criteria described in the general marking principles for this type of question.*	12

Question		Detailed marking principles	Max mark
2.	**(b)**	**(continued)**	
		Possible approaches to answering the question:	
		Most electors today obtain their political information from the media (either 'old media' such as newspapers or TV or 'new media' such as the internet or social media) and as such the media plays an important part in shaping the views of the electorate. For example, the stories that newspapers select or their choice of headlines, pictures or editorials can all have a 'drip, drip' effect on readers, influencing their politics over time. In the UK General Election of 2010 the Sun's and other newspapers' repeated criticism of Labour leader Gordon Brown was said to have cost Labour votes. Politicians and political parties would certainly agree with this view that newspapers influence voters as they often aim to keep newspaper owners or editors 'on side'. However, it has been argued that the influence of newspapers has been overstated. For example, many readers are unaware of, or ignore the political stance of their newspaper. It may also be the case that newspapers, such as the Sun, instead of influencing voters in 2010, switched its support to the Conservatives only when it became clear that Labour would lose.	
		(5 marks, one relevant point with a fully developed explanation and accurate, up-to-date and relevant exemplification plus evaluative comment)	
		The public perception of a party's leader and its policies can influence voting behaviour. For example, Gordon Brown had a poor public image (dour and distant) as Prime Minister before the 2010 General Election. Incidents such as 'bigotgate', when Gordon Brown accused a Labour supporter of bigotry, only served to make his image worse with Labour going on to lose. On the other hand, the Sun and many other newspapers portrayed David Cameron as young and fresh and it is argued by some that this helped the Conservatives defeat Labour.	
		In Scotland, the image of Alex Salmond has been good. Salmond has often been seen as being energetic, competent and statesmanlike. Even when the Sun newspaper attacked the SNP and Salmond in the 2007 Scottish Parliament Election, the SNP went on to become the largest party with Salmond as the new First Minister demonstrating that image is sometimes more important than newspaper support.	
		The 2011 Scottish Parliament election also highlights the importance of the party leader having a positive public image. Labour leader Iain Gray was accused of lacking personality and being dull. At one point on the campaign trail, he was forced into a shop to avoid awkward questions from members of the public. This seriously undermined his reputation. Gray's image therefore badly contrasted with that of Salmond and was said to have switched voters away from Labour to the SNP. At the 2011 Scottish Parliament election the SNP took the largest share of the vote and returned enough MSPs to form a majority government.	
		(6 marks, one relevant point with a fully developed explanation, accurate, up-to-date and relevant exemplification plus extended evaluative comment)	
		Overall, there are many different interlinked factors that affect voting behaviour. Some factors such as social class, age and geography overlap and are therefore difficult to measure separately. However, it clear that these long-term factors taken together continue to be an important influence on voting behaviour even if dealignment has reduced the importance of class-based voting. In the same way, it is difficult to measure the overall influence of the media/new media on voting behaviour. There is little doubt that people gain most of their political information from the media but it is impossible to identify one aspect or another of the media, e.g. the newspaper a voter reads, as being the single most important reason why they support any one party. However, most political commentators would agree that as the media becomes an ever greater influence in people's lives it is expected that the influence of the media, particularly new media, will increase.	
		(4 marks, overall evaluative comment that addresses the question)	

Section 2 — Social Issues in the UK

Question		Detailed marking principles	Max mark
1.		**Selectivity**	8
		Examples of the types of evidence that support the view include:	
		• Source A: Nicola Sturgeon argues that it is no coincidence that as the affordability of alcohol has plummeted in recent decades, alcohol-related deaths have increased and the SNP claims that MUP would lead to 1,200 fewer hospital admissions. *(2 marks)*	
		• Source A: Areas of deprivation have witnessed the highest increase in chronic liver disease (associated with the abuse of alcohol). Link to Source C: Glasgow areas of Maryhill and Shettleston have serious alcohol-related death rate — Shettleston 76 per 100,000 compared to 11 in Eastwood. *(2 marks)*	
		• BMA supports MUP and claims alcohol is a huge health and social problem for Scotland. Link to Source B: Almost 700 Scots per 100,000 were admitted to hospital with an alcohol-related diagnosis. *(1 mark)*	
		• Source A: While there has been a reduction in alcohol-related hospital admission and alcohol deaths it is still a very serious problem. Link to Source B: in 2011-12 almost 1,000 males were discharged from hospital with an alcohol-related illness. *(2 marks)*	
		• Any other relevant point.	
		Examples of types of evidence that does not support the view include:	
		• Source A: SWA states that there is no concrete evidence to support the reduction in number of alcohol-related admissions. *(1 mark)*	
		• Source A: Present action by the Scottish Government is already having an impact with the number of alcohol-related deaths falling from 1,500 in 2003 to just over 1,200 in 2012. *(1 mark)*	
		• Again alcohol-related hospitals admissions have declined over recent years so MUP is not necessary. Link to Source B: the overall number of alcohol-related hospital admissions/discharges has decreased from about 700 in 2008 to about 640 in 2012. *(2 marks)*	
		• Any other relevant point.	
		Overall comment (Up to 2 marks available):	
		The evidence supports the view to a large extent as:	
		• The alcohol-related deaths are highest in the poorest areas and as such the impact of MUP will have the greatest impact in these areas and lead to fewer admissions.	
		• While Source A and Source B show that the numbers of alcohol-related deaths and hospital discharges are declining, it is still a very serious problem as highlighted in Source C.	
		Comment on the origin or reliability of the source (Up to 2 marks available):	
		• Source A — "various" sources – extent of adaption not known. Source therefore not totally reliable.	
		• Source B is official health figures from the Scottish Government and are reliable and up-to-date.	
		• Source C is official health figures from the Office of National Statistics and are reliable and up-to-date.	
		On balance, the information is largely reliable.	
2.	(a)	**Analyse**	12
		Credit responses that make reference to:	
		• Evidence of social inequality as it affects a relevant group	
		• Analysis of the impact of social inequality on this group	
		Credit reference to aspects of the following:	
		• Impact on income and employment – poverty rates for Asian British and black British higher than white British; unemployment rates higher for ethnic minorities	
		• Impact on education – underperformance of black British students	
		• Impact of discrimination – direct and indirect discrimination	
		• Equality Act 2010	
		• Impact on health and housing	
		• Credit also accurate reference to other groups, e.g. women, people with disabilities, those on a low income	
		Any other valid point that meets the criteria described in the general marking principles for this type of question.	

Question		Detailed marking principles	Max mark
2.	**(a)**	**(continued)**	
		Possible approaches to answering the question:	
		In general, ethnic minorities suffer poorer health than whites; coronary heart disease and diabetes disproportionately affect the Asian population. Death rates from heart disease of 20–30-year-old Asians are twice as high compared to the general population. Black people are three times more likely to be diagnosed with schizophrenia. *(3 marks, accurate and developed point, exemplified with analytical/evaluative comment)*	
		Many ethnic minorities live in deprived inner-city areas, and living in sub-standard homes surrounded by poorly maintained amenities maintains social inequality. Ethnic minorities are geographically concentrated in larger urban areas, i.e. ethnic minorities tend only to live in large cities. They are not evenly dispersed throughout the country with 50% of all ethnic minorities contained in Greater London. In Scotland ethnic minorities make up more than 12% of the urban Glasgow population. Significantly 70% of all people who belong to an ethnic minority live in the 88 most deprived areas of the UK. Deprivation partially explains health inequality as death rates from heart disease of 20–30-year-old Asians are twice as high compared to the general population. *(5 marks, accurate and developed point, exemplified with extended analytical/evaluative comment)*	
		Educational inequalities do not apply to all ethnic minorities. In England, black, Bangladeshi and Pakistani pupils typically achieve less well than other pupils both in primary and secondary school, e.g. 50% of white pupils achieved 5 or more GCSEs, whereas only 37% of black and 30% of Pakistani pupils did so. However, those of Indian and Chinese origin outperformed white pupils with respective figures of 62% and 70%. Black Caribbean pupils are also more likely to be excluded as only 12 out of every 10,000 white pupils were excluded in England/Wales. For black Caribbean it was 38, Pakistani 8, Bangladeshi 6 and Indian 3. However, ethnic minorities are more likely to stay on at school – 85% do, compared to 67% of whites – but less likely to get a job at 16, perhaps due to some employers being less likely to employ people from a minority background.	
		Free meals statistics in England highlight that white children from poor backgrounds also experience social inequality. White pupils (16%) are far more likely than any other race to receive free school meals – Indian pupils only 4%, black Caribbean 8%. Socially, this means that many ethnic minorities have a better status than whites because they are financially better off and are therefore perhaps able to afford a healthier diet. *(8 marks, two separate accurate points, with description, explanation and exemplification plus extended analytical comment)*	
	(b)	**Analyse**	12
		Credit responses that make reference to:	
		• Policies to reduce social inequality • Analysis of the aims of different policies which aim to reduce social inequality	
		Credit reference to aspects of the following:	
		• Labour Government reforms: Welfare to Work – 300 000 extra lone mothers have found work; Job Centre Plus and JSA, Working Tax and Child Tax Credits: National Minimum Wage. 1.3 million workers will benefit from NMW.	
		• Coalition promise in 2010 to increase the state pension every year either by inflation, average earnings or a minimum of 2.5 % whichever is the highest — proportion of pensioners living in poverty has declined from 37% in 1991 to 14% by 2011.	
		• Welfare Reform Act 2012 — Coalition Government view is that work is the way out of poverty and recent welfare reforms will end dependency culture. Introduction of Jobseeker sanctions, £500 per week benefit cap reduction in housing benefit and removal of spare-room subsidy; Single Works programme; Help to Buy scheme.	
		• Groups such as the Joseph Rowntree Trust argue that welfare reforms/cuts penalise the poor and that child poverty will increase. Also argue that millions of working people are so low paid that they have drifted into poverty.	
		• Scottish Government policies — free prescriptions and free eye tests restored as universal benefit; retention of EMA for young Scots in school or college (scrapped in England by Coalition Government); Free school meals primary 1–3 introduced January 2015 in Scotland and 2014 in England; Equally Well report and policies to tackle poverty; Bedroom Tax to be abolished in Scotland; no student charges for Higher Education unlike England and Wales; and Opportunities for All scheme.	
		Any other valid point that meets the criteria described in the general marking principles for this type of question.	

Question		Detailed marking principles	Max mark
2.	(b)	**(continued)**	
		Possible approaches to answering the question:	
		Government welfare policies try to improve the employment opportunities of the unemployed and reduce social inequality. The Single Work Programme replaced New Deal. Now people claiming JSA can be referred instantly to SWP, do not have to wait 6 months. Claimants can access advice/training e.g. IT literacy, work experience/job interview skills and filling out CV/application forms. It is designed to be 'tough on the job-shy but supportive of the job-ready'.	
		(3 marks undeveloped point with some analysis)	
		The National Minimum Wage (NMW) introduced by the Labour Government in 1999 aimed to tackle poverty pay and to reduce the number of people in working poverty. Over one million workers receive the NMW which is £6.50 an hour. NMW has reduced gender inequality as 10% of women benefit compared to 4% of men. A 2013 Low Pay Commission Report claims that thanks to NMW the gap between ethnic minority workers and white workers has been significantly reduced. However the significant rise in food and utility prices has led to a campaign for NMW to be replaced with the Living Wage. The Joseph Rowntree Foundation suggests that the gap between NMW and the income needed to pay for a basic household budget has widened. Groups who support the Living Wage argue that employees in London need to be paid £ 8.80 (£7.65 outside London) to enable workers to have a decent wage. Many employers such as Aviva have introduced the Living Wage, however, the Coalition Government has no intention to introduce legislation to make a Living Wage compulsory.	
		(5 marks, accurate and developed point, exemplified with analytical/evaluative comment)	
		Government welfare policies try to improve the employment opportunities of the unemployed and reduce social inequality The Single Work Programme replaced New Deal. Now people claiming JSA can be referred instantly to SWP, do not have to wait 6 months. Claimants can access advice/training e.g. IT literacy, work experience/job interview skills and filling out CV/application forms. It is designed to be 'tough on the job-shy but supportive of the job-ready'. In total from June 1, 2012, to March 31, 2014 there were 1.20 million referred to the Work Programme and 1.16 million attached to a job provider e.g. Serco. A job provider is a company which works for the government to try to get people into employment. Staff from private companies e.g. Serco can get £300 bonuses per month if they reach their target and get enough people into employment and reach their targets. Just one in 10 people have been helped back to work by the government's £5 billion flagship scheme, leading to accusations that the programme is 'worse than doing nothing'. A total of 130,000 of the 1.2million people who have joined the Work Programme since June 2011 are now in employment. Just one in 20 people on sickness benefit who were on the programme found work. The target was one in six. In 2014, unemployment rates were 7.6% — the lowest rate for 3 years.	
		(8 marks, range of knowledge, description/explanation, exemplification and extended analytical/ evaluative comment)	
	(c)	**Analyse**	12
		Credit responses that make reference to:	
		• Policies which aim to reduce re-offending • Analysis of policies aimed to reduce re-offending	
		Credit reference to aspects of the following:	
		• Educational qualifications and work/drug/alcohol programmes in prison. • The prison population is now double what it was when Ken Clarke was Home Secretary in the early 1990s. The Conservatives accepted in 2010 that prisons were not the solution to crime and that alternatives to prisons should be expanded. The SNP Government also accepts that alternatives to prisons should be used for short-term prisoners. • Prison numbers are still rising, recidivist rates still increasing, rehabilitation not revolutionising penal system. Effective rehabilitation projects still small-scale. Many are only accessible to long-term prisoners. • Alternatives to prison, community payback orders, electronic tagging and restorative justice. • Early intervention programmes for young offenders/work of Children's Hearings System.	
		Any other valid point that meets the criteria described in the general marking principles for this type of question.	

Question		Detailed marking principles	Max mark
2.	(c)	**(continued)**	
		Possible approaches to answering the question:	
		All political parties now accept that prisons are failing to prevent re-offending especially for short-term prisons and that alternatives are the way forward. Three-quarters of prisoners on a short-term sentence re-offend within 2 years. Too many people in Britain get sent to jail and the UK sends more people to prison per head of population compared to most European countries.	
		(2 marks, KU)	
		Prisons can only work if they achieve their central aim of rehabilitation. Education is an important aspect of rehabilitation. According to the SPS, inmates spend only 21% of their time in educational classes delivering literacy. However, it also reports that 18,406 inmates were awarded VEQ in 2012/13. This is an increase from 16,673 the previous year. Prisoner employability prospects have increased only marginally from 10% (2012) of inmates to 11% (2013). Only half the prisoners in training prisons felt that their education would help them on release, and even fewer (42%) felt that they had gained useful vocational skills and 36% of people leaving prison go into education, training or employment.	
		(5 marks, description/explanation, exemplification and evaluative comment)	
		Alternatives to prison are now used across the UK and one such policy in Scotland is Community Payback Orders (CPOs). A court can order between 80 and 300 hours of supervised work which must be completed within six months of the date of sentence. Offenders avoid the stigma of imprisonment and the possibility of falling into bad company and the criminal culture of the prison. Again, offenders can remain with their families and possibly prevent the break-up of the family and children being put into care. This policy does not only reduce re-offending but prevents the next generation of vulnerable children possibly ending up in jail – a quarter of prisoners in prison had been in care as a child. CPOs also enable the offender to make restitution for their crime by improving their community. CPO is also far less costly to implement than a short prison sentence and the money saved can be reinvested into properly financed rehabilitation programmes in prison. Unfortunately many offenders fail to comply with the order and only one-third of CPOs are completed. So, many offenders go back to court and receive a prison sentence and no financial savings are made nor are the aims of CPO achieved.	
		(7 marks, knowledge, description/explanation, exemplification and extended analytical/ evaluative comment)	
	(d)	**Analyse**	12
		Credit responses that make reference to:	
		• Cost to society including physical, emotional and financial	
		• Impact on individuals, communities, business and wider society	
		Credit reference to aspects of the following:	
		• Emotional/physical impact of crime on individuals	
		• Social/financial cost to communities	
		• Financial implications on individuals, communities, businesses and wider society	
		Any other valid point that meets the criteria described in the general marking principles for this type of question.	
		Possible approaches to answering the question:	
		The impact of crime on society can be far-reaching especially for the victim. For some there may be physical damage or harm. Violent crime can bring out deep reactions in people such as anxiety and depression. Elderly people feel especially vulnerable and may be afraid to go out at night.	
		(2 marks, evaluative point)	
		Crime can have a hugely negative impact on local communities. High crime levels can contribute to 'environmental poverty' that is areas with high crime often suffer from vandalism, graffiti and create fear for people who live there. They may suffer depression and anxiety which may impact on their health. Living in these areas will increase house and car insurance costs and may create financial difficulties. Fear of crime also deters people from using public facilities such as parks and public transport.	
		(3 marks, evaluative point)	

Question		Detailed marking principles	Max mark
2.	(d)	**(continued)**	
		As well as the emotional and physical impact of crime, there is an obvious financial cost to taxpayers. In 2013–14 the Scottish Government spent £2.5 billion on criminal justice. This is the third highest area of spending after health and local government. The Scottish court system costs £73 million and the Scottish prison services £346 million. It is estimated that the annual cost of housing a prisoner is £40,000. This is money that the Scottish Government could have spent on new hospitals and schools. In 2013, the Guardian newspaper reported that retail crime costs the sector £1.6 billion per year. There are on average 2 million incidents of shoplifting a year in the UK. Relatively new crime such as Identity theft cost the UK £2.7 billion a year. These crimes are not 'victimless' as the consumer pays for these later through higher charges.	
		(6 marks, two relevant points, detailed and accurate exemplification plus extended comment)	

Section 3 — International Issues

Question		Detailed marking principles	Max mark
1.	(a)	**To what extent**	20
		Credit responses that make reference to:	
		• Evidence of social and economic inequality	
		• Analysis of social and economic inequality as it affects different individuals or groups	
		• Balanced overall evaluative comment on the extent to which individuals or groups experience social and economic inequality	
		• A clear, coherent line of argument	
		Credit reference to aspects of the following:	
		• Social inequalities may refer to education, health and health care, crime, etc.	
		• Economic inequalities may refer to wealth, employment/unemployment, income, etc.	
		• Candidates may integrate social and economic factors as this is an acceptable approach	
		• Social factors such as education, health, housing and crime; economic factors such as employment/unemployment, wealth distribution and poverty based on racial divide.	
		• For example, evidence of educational inequalities between all black township and rural schools and middle-class integrated schools in terms of matriculation results and school amenities; regional inequalities, for example, between schools in Western Cape and Limpopo; evidence of progress, for example, impact of BEE legislation, entry to higher education and improved literacy rates, modernisation of schools and improved matriculation results.	
		• Evidence of health inequalities between wealthy South Africans with access to private health care and majority of blacks using an over-subscribed national health service — issues of HIV-Aids and impact on poorer South Africans and racial and provincial health inequalities. Evidence of progress — primary health care reforms, Mandela sandwich and access to clean water for more than 12 million.	
		• Evidence of economic inequalities between wealthy whites and majority of blacks and between provinces. While white unemployment is about 7% it is officially 30 % for black South Africans and an average black person earns 40 % of an average white person's income. Evidence of progress — impact of BEE legislation and creation of a wealthy black educated middle class (Black Diamonds); expansion of social grant to 13 million South Africans.	
		Any other valid point that meets the criteria described in the general marking principles for this type of question.	

Question		Detailed marking principles	Max mark
1.	(a)	**(continued)**	

(continued)

Possible approaches to answering the question — World Power: USA

- Education inequalities. According to the 2010 Census, 34% of Americans have been educated to tertiary level (college/university) but 53% of Asians have completed university. However, inequalities are still evident as only 19% of blacks and 13% of Hispanics have a degree.
- Health inequalities — 16% of whites, 21% of blacks and 32% of Asians have no health insurance. Similarly, 17% Hispanics have no health insurance, 11% of Asian, 13% black but only 7% of whites.
- Housing inequalities — whites are still predominately located in 'vanilla suburbs', i.e. affluent suburban areas on the outskirts of towns and cities. By contrast, African Americans and Hispanics are generally based in deprived inner-city areas known as ghettos and Hispanics in 'barrios'.
- Economic inequalities — blacks (36%) and Hispanic Americans (31%) are more likely to live in poverty compared to whites (22%); income inequality — whites ($62,000) earn on average per annum more than African Americans ($38,000) and Hispanics ($40,000).

Any other valid point that meets the criteria described in the general marking principles for this type of question.

Possible approaches to answering the question — World Power: South Africa

One issue of social inequality is education provision. COSATU has described black education thus: 'Many schools are no more than dumping grounds for children — unsafe, bleak, uninspiring places where violence and abuse are rife'. There is a teacher shortage in township schools. 50,000 teachers have died in recent years due to AIDS and class sizes in township schools are often over 50 pupils. So educational inequality is still a major problem in South Africa.
(3 marks, accurate point with explanation, exemplification and analytical/evaluative comment)

Despite 20 years of black majority rule the legacy of apartheid is still reflected in health provision. Many whites have private health cover while only about 10% of black South Africans are covered. State hospitals are underfunded and suffer from staff shortages. There are also significant regional inequalities between the provinces and between urban and rural communities. Gauteng and Western Cape are the richest provinces and have the best health provision. While there are 37 doctors per 100,000 of the population in the Western Cape, it falls to only 11 in Limpopo. Malnutrition is a major problem in rural areas and there have been outbreaks of cholera in KwaZulu-Natal. The areas with the poorest health provision have the highest number of HIV/Aids sufferers. There are also significant differences between the races — 13% of black South Africans suffer AIDS compared to 1% of whites. As such, health inequalities are not just racial but also regional.
(6 marks, range of knowledge, description/explanation, exemplification and balanced analytical/ evaluative comment)

Affirmative Action legislation such as Employment Equity Act and BEE legislation which gives preferential treatment to black South Africans has helped to create a better educated and well paid black workforce. Unfortunately only about 10% of blacks benefit from this policy. Critics of these policies argue that while it has helped the creation of over three million wealthy blacks it has brought little social and economic benefits to the remaining 90 % of blacks. Many still live in informal settlements with poor amenities, high crime and massive unemployment. In fact since 1994 inequality between the poorest and richest blacks has widened. It has encouraged 'crony capitalism' and a culture of entitlement that breeds corruption. This means that many ANC politicians use their political influence and contacts to become rich. BEE is inefficient as it promotes many workers to jobs they are not capable of doing. This has led to schools not receiving textbooks or funds to pay the fees of poor students.

(6 marks, range of knowledge, description/explanation, exemplification and balanced analytical/ evaluative comment)

It is clear that the majority of black South Africans and a minority of whites still experience significant social and economic inequalities. For those who remain in the informal settlements, life is the same as it was during the apartheid years — segregated communities and schools, limited education and employment prospects. However progress has been made for those living in the settled townships with new homes, clean water and electricity. The creation of a wealthy black middle class offers hope for the future despite criticism of BEE.

(4 marks, balanced overall comments with a clear line of argument)

Question		Detailed marking principles	Max mark
1.	(b)	**Discuss**	20
		Credit responses that make reference to:	
		• The political system of the world power	
		• Analysis of the ways in which the political system guarantees and protects the rights of all of its citizens	
		• Balanced overall evaluative comment on the extent to which the political system protects the rights of all of its citizens	
		• A clear, coherent line of argument	
		Credit reference to aspects of the following — World Power: South Africa	
		• South Africa is a well-established democracy with an extensive Bill of Rights, fair and free elections, high voter turnout, a fair electoral system and many political parties to vote for.	
		• Regular elections are held every 5 years and the President can only serve 2 terms. The Party List electoral system is highly proportionate as the percentage of votes a party wins will be roughly the same as the number of seats they get in parliament.	
		• At the 2014 General Election, voters could vote for a range of parties — ANC led by Jacob Zuma and Democratic Alliance led by Helen Zille. There were also seven new parties such as the Economic Freedom Fighters.	
		• One view is that the ANC has too much power and that South Africa is moving towards a one-party state. This makes it far from being fair and democratic.	
		• ANC controls eight out of the nine provinces and only the DA in Western Cape offers an alternative.	
		Any other valid point that meets the criteria described in the general marking principles for this type of question.	
		Possible approaches to answering the question — World Power: USA	
		• USA has a written constitution which protects the rights of its citizens	
		• Democracy is based on the separation of powers between executive, legislature and judiciary	
		• Supreme Court interprets the Constitution and can declare actions of the President and Congress illegal	
		• A federal system that divides powers between the federal government and states	
		• A free media with free opportunity to join pressure groups and to protest against government actions	
		• Numerous elections at all levels to ensure government accountability	
		• The separation of powers prevents laws being passed that are supported by the majority — President Obama cannot get his gun reforms passed by Congress	
		• The poor and minorities feel that politics is a rich man's club. Again, concern over the failure to renew the Voting Rights Act.	
		• Government surveillance impacts on the rights of the individual.	
		Any other valid point that meets the criteria described in the general marking principles for this type of question.	
		Possible approaches to answering the question — World Power: South Africa	
		The electoral system strengthens the President's powers and stifles debate and opposition within the ruling party. The Party List system gives President Zuma great power as he must approve the ANC candidates. This means that ANC politicians are more loyal to their leader than to the voters as they fear being moved down the list. In the past ANC politicians have been removed for criticising ANC policies. Zuma fired Trevor Ngwane for criticising his privatisation policies. The President appoints not only his ministers but also eight of the nine premiers of the provincial governments.	
		(4 marks, range of knowledge, description/explanation, exemplification and analytical/evaluative comment)	
		South Africa has all the features of a successive democracy with national elections held every 5 years and voters allowed to choose from a range of political parties. A Party List PR system exists which enables a range of political parties to be represented in the National Assembly. It has a written constitution which includes a Bill of Rights and also provides for an independent judiciary to interpret the legality of government actions.	
		(3 marks, accurate and developed point, with some analytical/evaluative comment)	

Question		Detailed marking principles	Max mark
1.	(b)	**(continued)**	
		South Africa has all the features of a successive democracy with national elections held every 5 years and voters allowed to choose from a range of political parties. A Party List PR system exists which enables a range of political parties to be represented in the National Assembly. However this PR system weakens the formation of a strong opposition party as it encourages new parties to be created — if they win 1% of the votes they will obtain four seats. It has a written constitution which includes a Bill of Rights and also provides for an independent judiciary to interpret the legality of government actions. However the constitution discriminates against whites as Article 9.2 states that legislation can be enforced that penalises whites, such as BEE legislation.	
		(5 marks, accurate and developed point, with detailed analytical/evaluative comment)	
		To conclude, it can be argued that South Africa's political system is democratic as free and fair elections are held and the public can choose from a range of political parties. It has a liberal constitution and the people's rights are protected by a still independent judiciary — the Constitutional Court. It still has a free press and the government can be criticised and challenged. However, the domination, corruption and arrogance of the ANC could lead to a one-party state. Jacob Zuma has stated that the ANC will rule 'until Jesus returns'. Legislation has been passed through parliament to weaken the freedom of the press and to prevent newspapers from exposing the corruption of the ANC leadership. Zuma's control of the Public Prosecution Department and state security are worrying signs of a step towards dictatorship. Respected figures such as Desmond Tutu have openly attacked the corruption of the ANC and endorse the view that there are two types of ANC leaders — those who were in jail (under white rule) and those who should be in jail.	
		(4 marks, balanced conclusion with detailed evaluative comment)	
	(c)	**Discuss**	20
		Credit responses that make reference to:	
		• Details/background of a world issue • Analysis of the social, economic and political factors that gave rise to the world issue • Balanced overall evaluative comment on the causes of the world issue • A clear, coherent line of argument	
		Credit reference to aspects of the following:	
		• World issue: international terrorism • World issue: nuclear proliferation • World issue: crisis in Ukraine • World issue: development in Africa • World issue: borders disputes — Arab-Israeli • World issue: global economic crisis	
		Any other valid point that meets the criteria described in the general marking principles for this type of question.	
		Possible approaches to answering the question:	
		Lack of development in African countries, particularly those below the Sahara, is an issue of world concern. Africa is made up of 54 countries and of these 34 are classified as being the least developed nations in the world. Seventy per cent of Africa's population subsist on less than $2 dollars a day. A complex combination of political, social and economic factors interact to impede development. Widespread corruption or civil war, a lack of basic infrastructure and natural disasters and the spread of infectious diseases such as HIV/AIDS and now Ebola, can all impact on development.	
		(3 marks, accurate point with explanation and analysis)	
		Poor health is a major cause of lack of development in many African countries. HIV/AIDS has become one the biggest problems facing people in Africa in recent years with an estimated 26 million adults and children suffering from HIV/AIDS. During 2014, an estimated 1.5 million Africans died from AIDS and there are about 12 million orphaned African children. In 2012, AIDS killed more than 2.5 million adults and 610,000 children. Swaziland with 26% and Lesotho with 23% have the highest percentages of people infected. HIV/AIDS places a huge burden on societies in Africa. The death of skilled workers and professionals such as teachers and doctors deprives the labour market of its most important workers. The economic impact on families and services is huge — many families lose their income provider and the cost of anti-AIDS drugs drains the health service.	
		(5 marks, accurate and developed point, exemplified with extended analytical/evaluative comment)	

Question		Detailed marking principles	Max mark
1.	**(c)**	**(continued)**	
		Political systems impact on development. Many African states are kleptocracies where leaders use their power to benefit themselves by stealing public funds and/or aid money, accepting bribes or getting advantages in business. The late Nigerian dictator Sani Abacha stole between $1 billion and $3 billion in the space of 5 years. All this corruption diverts money away from aid projects and essential services. The Ugandan Health Minister is suspected of stealing $1 million of international aid money that was intended to fund development projects. However, not all African governments are inept and dishonest. The Mo Ibrahim Prize for Achievement in African Leadership is awarded to leaders who have records of honesty and integrity, e.g. Joaquim Chissano (former president of Mozambique) and Festus Mogae, former president of Botswana, are both former winners. The famine now being experienced in South Sudan is a direct result of poor and corrupt leadership by its rulers. They squandered the income from the oil fields on weapons and personal wealth. The result was a civil war between the ruling factions in the government and social and economic disaster for the people.	
		(6 marks, accurate and developed point, exemplified with balanced extended analytical/ evaluative comment)	
		To conclude, world issues such as lack of development in Africa are caused by a range of political, social and economic factors such as lack of education, trading cash crops, corrupt political regimes and poor health systems. One reason that the 2014 Ebola outbreak has been so deadly in Guinea, Liberia and Sierra Leone is that their respective health services could not cope. South Sudan is a very good example of the way a new country rich in oil and provided with substantial financial support from the international agencies can descend into chaos and famine.	
		(3 marks, overall conclusion with overall evaluative, analytical comment that addresses the question)	
	(d)	**To what extent**	20
		Credit responses that make reference to:	
		• Details/background of a world issue • Analysis of the ways international organisations have attempted to resolve a world issue • Balanced overall evaluative comment on the extent to which international organisations have resolved a world issue • A clear, coherent line of argument	
		Credit reference to aspects of the following:	
		• World issue — international terrorism (UN/NATO) • World Issue — nuclear weapons — North Korea and nuclear proliferation (UN) • World Issue — Russia expansion in Eastern Europe (UN, NATO , EU) • World Issue — crisis in Euro-zone (EU) • World issue — development in Africa (UN and agencies, EU, World Bank, AU) • World issue — land disputes — Arab-Israeli (UN)	
		Any other valid point that meets the criteria described in the general marking instructions for this kind of question.	
		Possible approaches to the question:	
		NATO has brought peace and security to the new states that once made up Yugoslavia. The break-up of Yugoslavia led to ethnic conflict between Serbians, Croatians and Bosnians. NATO restored peace by sending in peacekeeping troops and using air strikes. At present, NATO still retains some troops in Kosovo which lies between Serbia and Albania. Tension is still very high in this region.	
		(2 marks, KU with evaluative comment)	
		The United Nations has held Security Council (SC) debates on the crisis in Ukraine. In the case of Crimea declaring itself part of Russia, a Security Council debate was held but no action taken against Russia. Putin, the Russian leader, declared that a referendum had been held and the people of Crimea had voted in large numbers to leave Ukraine and become citizens of Russia. When Russia invaded Georgia in 2008 and occupied South Ossetia, no military action was taken by international organisations.	
		(3 marks KU)	
		The United Nations has held Security Council (SC) debates on the crisis in Ukraine. In the case of Crimea declaring itself part of Russia, a Security Council debate was held but no action taken against Russia. Putin, the Russian leader, declared that a referendum had been held and the people of Crimea had voted in large numbers to leave Ukraine and become citizens of Russia.	

Question		Detailed marking principles	Max mark
1.	(d)	**(continued)**	
		Again, when the Malaysia Airlines plane was shot down by a Russian-made missile in July 2014 an emergency SC meeting was held to discuss the death of the 298 passengers. It was agreed that the UN would investigate the causes of the crash and take appropriate action once all evidence was recovered from the site. Unfortunately, the pro-Russian rebels who most likely shot down the plane destroyed much of the evidence and it may never be possible to prove beyond all doubt that Russia was to blame. All the permanent members of the SC have a veto and can block any action against them. This makes it very difficult to resolve world issues and weakens the effectiveness of the UN to maintain peace and security.	
		(6 marks, accurate and developed point, exemplified with analytical/evaluative comment)	
		A range of international organisations — United Nations, NATO and EU — are involved in trying to solve the present crisis in Ukraine but with very limited success. Even if the Security Council decided that Russian troops are fighting in Ukraine and were involved in the shooting down of the civilian plane, Russia can use its veto to prevent action. The US and NATO have ruled out military action to defend Ukraine even if the Russians invade Ukraine. Limited sanctions have been imposed on Russia for its occupation of Crimea. EU and US banking restrictions have had some impact on the Russian economy. Ukraine is not a member of NATO and there is no obligation on NATO to defend Ukraine.	
		(4 marks, overall conclusion with overall evaluative, analytical comment that addresses the question)	

HIGHER FOR CfE MODERN STUDIES
MODEL PAPER 2

Section 1 — Democracy in Scotland and UK

Question		Detailed marking principles	Max mark
1.		**Conclusion** Possible responses include: **The representation of women in the Scottish Parliament compared to the UK Parliament** • Women are better represented in the Scottish Parliament compared to the UK Parliament. *(1 mark)* Source A states around 1 in 4 MPs are women whereas around a third of MSPs are female. *(1 mark)* This is backed up by Source B which shows in 2010 only 22.3% of MPs were women compared to 34.9% of MSPs who were women in 2011. *(1 mark)* • Women's representation has increased in the UK Parliament whereas it has fallen in the Scottish Parliament. *(1 mark)* Source A states in 2010 women made up 1 in 4 MPs, up from 1 in 10 in 1992, in the UK Parliament whereas the number of MSPs is lower than when the Scottish Parliament was established in 1999. *(1 mark)* This is backed up by Source B which shows the percentage of female representation in UK Parliament has risen from 18.2% in 1997 to 22.3% in 2010 and in Scotland female MSP representation has fallen from 36% in 1999 to 34.9% in 2011. *(1 mark)* <div align="right">**(3 marks)**</div> **The representation of women in different political parties in Scotland and the UK** • Labour has the highest female representation in both Scotland and the UK. *(1 mark)* This is backed up by Source C which shows Labour has the most female MPs (86) which is 33% of all the Labour MPs. *(1 mark)* Source C also shows that although Labour does not have the highest number of female MSPs (17 compared to 18 for SNP), Labour is the party with the highest percentage of female MSPs at 46%. *(1 mark)* • The SNP has a good record on female representation in the Scottish Cabinet and in the number of female MSPs. *(1 mark)* Source C shows the SNP have the highest number of female MSPs (18) although this is a lower percentage (26%) compared to Labour (46%) and the Conservatives (40%). *(1 mark)* Source A also states 40% of Scottish Cabinet Ministers are female although the percentage of SNP female MSPs has fallen from over 40% to under 30% since 1999. *(1 mark)* <div align="right">**(3 marks)**</div> Overall, it could be concluded that women remain under-represented in both Scottish and UK politics, having less than half the representatives at any level anywhere in the UK. *(1 mark)* However, the picture is changing and it is not the same across Scotland and the UK. For example, the representation of women has increased in the UK Parliament although it has fallen marginally in both the Scottish Parliament and the Welsh Assembly. *(1 mark)* *Any other valid point* <div align="right">**(2 marks)**</div>	8
2.	(a)	**Evaluate** Credit responses that make reference to: • Evidence of social class as a factor influencing voting behaviour • An evaluation of the importance of social class as one factor influencing voting behaviour Credit reference to aspects of the following (Scottish and/or UK dimensions): • Work of Butler & Stokes, Pulzer & Denver. According to Butler and Stokes (1974) most voters voted on the basis of social class in the 1950s & 1960s: 2/3 of the working class (as defined then) voted Labour and 4/5 of the middle class (as defined then) voted Conservative. • Partisan de-alignment has weakened party identification. Now more difficult to define electorate simply as' working class' or 'middle class'. Working-class people now have more in common with traditional middle class, e.g. non-trade union member, non-manual work, more likely to enter tertiary education, etc. • At the 2010 General Election some evidence that around half of voters still voted along class lines. Multi-party politics has also blurred lines with SNP in Scotland and UKIP throughout UK. • Factors other than social class, e.g. media/new media, gender/ethnicity, geography, leadership, issues also influence voting behaviour e.g. live televised debates by party leaders, issues, such as spending on welfare services, defence and foreign affairs such as Iraq and EU policies. • Influence of tactical voting.	12

Question		Detailed marking principles	Max mark
2.	(a)	**(continued)** • Scottish dimension — success of SNP in Scottish Parliament elections highlights the decline of class voting in Scotland although a strong factor in the 2010 General Election in Scotland. *Any other valid point that meets the criteria described in the general marking principles for this type of question.* **Possible approaches to answering the question (Scottish & UK dimensions):** *Until the early 1980s, social class was viewed as the most important influence in voting behaviour. P.J. Pulzer stated: 'Class is the basis of British party politics. All else is embellishment and detail.' Therefore, social class was believed to have a profound influence over voting behaviour. Labour was closely associated with the then working class and trade unions and the Conservatives with upper and middle classes and business.* **(2 marks, one relevant point plus limited evaluative comment)** *Evidence suggests that social class has diminished in importance as a result of a decline in class party identification referred to as partisan dealignment. In the 1960s, 44% of voters were 'very strong' supporters of the two main parties but by 2008 this figure had dropped to 12%. The rise in support for Liberal Democrats and SNP in Scotland provides further evidence of partisan dealignment. SNP ended Labour's dominance in the Scottish Parliament by winning both the 2007 and 2011 Scottish Parliament elections. SNP support is not based on social class.* **(3 marks, one relevant point with accurate and relevant exemplification plus limited evaluative and analytical comment)** *Social class remains an important factor especially in UK elections. Labour, as the party more supportive of policies that aid the poorest most, e.g. commitment to the Welfare State, remains the most popular party in the UK among lower-class voters (or D and E as defined today). The Conservatives, who favour lower tax and support for business, still have greater support among the middle/professional classes (A and B).* *Overall, in the 2010, General Election, 39% of ABC1s voted Conservative compared to 27% who voted Labour. Breaking this down, the areas traditionally associated with a strong working class — Scotland, Wales and north of England, voted more often for Labour. In Scotland, Labour actually increased its share of the vote in the 2010 General Election, clearly indicating the importance of social class.* **(4 marks, one relevant point with a fully developed explanation and accurate, up-to-date and relevant exemplification plus evaluative comment)** *It is clear that short-term factors such as image of party leaders are important. In the 2010 General Election, opinion polls were very critical of Gordon Brown's leadership. While 24% of the public regarded Cameron as having a great deal of personality, only 4% placed Gordon Brown in this category. At the 2011 Scottish Parliament elections, leadership was seen as a significant factor in influencing behaviour. Alex Salmond was regarded as the most competent politician to lead the country. In contrast, the Labour leader Iain Gray had a less favourable public persona. In both elections the leader with the poorest public image lost, suggesting that the image/competence of a party leader is a factor in voting behaviour.* **(4 marks, one relevant point with a fully developed explanation and accurate, up-to-date and relevant exemplification plus evaluative comment)** *To finish, social class may no longer be the dominant factor in voting behaviour as a result of partisan dealignment and the growing importance of short-term issues such as the media or the competence or image of party leaders. However, social class cannot be dismissed altogether as irrelevant. It is still an important influence especially in UK elections as many voters continue to vote along class lines.* **(2 marks overall evaluative comment that addresses the question)**	
	(b)	**Evaluate** **Credit responses that make reference to:** • The role of parliamentary representatives in the decision-making process • An evaluation of the important roles of parliamentary representatives in the decision-making process **Credit reference to aspects of the following (Scottish dimension):** • Debates, questions to ministers, motions and voting • Role of committees • Role and influence of Whips • Impact of a majority/minority government *Any other valid point that meets the criteria described in the general marking principles for this type of question.*	12

Question		Detailed marking principles	Max mark
2.	**(b)**	**(continued)**	
		Possible approaches to answering the question (Scottish dimension):	
		MSPs have a number of important roles in the Scottish Parliament. For example, an MSP may take part in a debate on one of the devolved powers such as education. MSPs may also work in committees where they may scrutinise the work of the Scottish Government.	
		(2 marks, two accurate but largely undeveloped points)	
		Committees play an important role in involving MSPs in decision-making with all legislation being considered by a committee. Committees, which are made up of small numbers of MSPs from different parties, can conduct inquiries, take on fact-finding visits and produce reports. They can also put forward their own proposals for new legislation (known as Committee Bills). However, after the 2011 election the SNP formed a majority government which makes it more difficult, in theory, for MSPs to influence government decision-making. The SNP no longer needs to build consensus with regard to the Budget or law-making as it did between 2007 and 2011. The SNP often dominates committees and the opposition parties claim it is now more difficult to call the Scottish Government to account.	
		(4 marks, accurate point with developed explanation, exemplification and evaluative comment)	
		In conclusion, MSPs do have a number of important roles to play in the Scottish Parliament. Despite a majority government, MSPs from opposition parties contribute to the development of legislation and can influence government decisions. The recent decision to delay the proposal for the ending of corroboration in legal cases was partly due to the influence of MSPs in the Justice Committee.	
		(2 marks, overall detailed evaluative comment that addresses the question)	
		Credit reference to aspects of the following (UK dimension):	
		• Debates, questions to ministers, motions and voting • Role and powers of committees • Role and influence of Whips • Impact of coalition government	
		Any other valid point that meets the criteria described in the general marking principles for this type of question.	
		Possible approaches to answering the question:	
		Law-making is an important role undertaken by parliamentary representatives as legislation must be approved by Parliament (House of Commons and House of Lords) before it becomes law.	
		(1 mark analysis/evaluative comment)	
		The House of Lords has no say in financial bills. Only the House of Commons decides, for example, on the Budget. For the most part, the government's financial proposals are rubber-stamped by MPs as the government of the day tends to have a working majority.	
		(2 marks, point plus analysis/evaluative comment)	
		It has been argued that the existence of the Conservative/Liberal Democrats Coalition Government has increased MPs' influence in government decision-making policies. This is because no one party has control of the House of Commons and there is a greater chance that policies proposed by the coalition may be challenged by MPs from one of the coalition parties. In 2012, the Conservative-Liberal Democrat Coalition Government, faced with a Conservative backbench revolt, dropped its plans to reform the House of Lords and in retaliation Liberal Democrat MPs opposed the Conservative proposal to reduce the number of MPs in the House of Commons. Another example was in 2013 when MPs voted against the government's proposed UK military action in Syria in response to Syria's use of chemical weapons on its own people.	
		(4 marks, accurate point with developed explanation and extended up-to-date exemplification plus evaluative comment)	
		To conclude, there are many important roles for parliamentary representatives in the UK Parliament. From law-making to scrutiny of the government, there are many opportunities for individual MPs to influence the decision-making process. At the present time, as there is a coalition government, it has been argued by some that this has given MPs more influence than in other years.	
		(2 marks, overall evaluative comment that addresses the question)	

Section 2 — Social Issues in the UK

Question		Detailed marking principles	Max mark
1.	(a)	**To what extent** **Credit responses that make reference to:** • Links between poverty and bad health • Analysis of a range of other factors that influence health • Balanced overall evaluative comment on the extent to which poverty is the most important factor influencing health • A clear, coherent line of argument **Credit reference to aspects of the following:** • Evidence of the link between poverty and poor health • Poor lifestyle choices including excess alcohol consumption, unhealthy diet, smoking and lack of exercise, drug misuse, etc. • Other factors: hereditary, gender, ethnicity, etc. • Failure to make best use of preventative care services • North–South divide in terms of health *Any other valid point that meets the criteria described in the general marking principles for this type of question.* **Possible approaches to answering the question:** *Many reports in Scotland and the UK have demonstrated the link between poor health and poverty. For example, the Equally Well Review of 2013 (second review of Equally Well, 2008) heard evidence that Glasgow and the West of Scotland were experiencing many more deaths than comparable cities and regions in the UK.* *(2 marks, accurate point with development)* *There are numerous official reports that link poverty and deprivation to poor health, from the Black Report of 1980 through to the Scottish Health Survey (SHS) 2012. The SHS 2012 report stated that males born in the most affluent parts of Scotland in 2011–12 could hope to reach the age of 70 years before suffering poor health. In contrast, males in the poorest areas would only reach, on average, 46 years of age. This highlights the massive health inequalities that exist in Scotland.* *(3 marks, accurate point with extended development)* *Poor lifestyle choices also contribute to bad health. Smoking, bad diet and excess alcohol consumption all play a part in affecting health. For example, despite the link between smoking and lung cancer, many Scots continue to smoke. Health statistics indicate that annually there are more than 1,300 smoking-related deaths in Scotland. Also, children in the most deprived parts of Scotland are twice as likely to be obese as those in the most affluent areas. Finally, for women attending antenatal clinics, 36% of those from the most deprived areas smoke, compared to 6% from wealthy areas. Therefore, it could be argued that it is not just poverty that affects health and that individual lifestyle choices also play a huge part. However, even if allowances are made for poor lifestyle choices amongst the most deprived groups, people on the lowest incomes are still more likely to die at a younger age or experience more ill health.* *(5 marks, accurate and developed point, exemplified with evaluative comment)* *Overall, poverty is the most important factor in influencing health. Unemployment and/or a low income limits choice in housing, diet, heating, clothing, etc. This puts a massive strain on individuals and their families and impacts greatly on physical and mental wellbeing. Since 2008 and the Equally Well report, the Scottish Government has recognised that poverty is the most important factor influencing health. Recently, the Scottish Government tried to reduce the impact of the 'bedroom tax' in Scotland by increasing support for those affected. This was a direct response to the impact of the 'bedroom tax' on many already very poor people.* *(4 marks, overall evaluative comment that addresses the question)*	20
	(b)	**Discuss** **Credit responses that make reference to:** • Aims of the Welfare State • Analysis of the ways in which government tries to meet the aims of the Welfare State • Balanced overall evaluative comment on the extent to which the Welfare State meet its aims • A clear, coherent line of argument	20

Question		Detailed marking principles	Max mark
1.	(b)	**(continued)**	

Credit reference to aspects of the following:

- The Welfare State provides social protection with the state taking the lead role in caring for the individual 'from the cradle to the grave'.
- Principle of universality with contributions from all.
- Designed to tackle 'Five Giant Evils' with creation of a Social Security system, NHS, social housing and expanded education. Today includes services for children.
- Pressures on Welfare State including ageing population, continuation of child poverty, higher expectations, etc.
- Impact of 'age of austerity' and coalition welfare reforms and cuts.
- NHS budgets protected across UK but remains 'free at the point of need'. Success of NHS but 'victim of its own success'. Implication of privatisation of services and opening of NHS in England to market forces.
- Differences within the UK, e.g. continuation of EMA in Scotland but not England. Tuition fees charged In England and Wales but not Scotland, etc.

Any other valid point that meets the criteria described in the general marking principles for this kind of question.

Possible approaches to answering the question:

The Welfare State was set up to provide a safety net in which the state would take responsibility to provide support for all those in need. The state would look after us "from the cradle to the grave" to provide free education and health and provide assistance for the unemployed, the elderly and the sick.

(2 marks, partly developed relevant point)

The Welfare State has, despite pressures on budgets, maintained its universal and means-tested benefits for the elderly. (Between 2012–15 over £70 billion of cuts have been made in public sector spending). The proportion of pensioners living in poverty has declined over the last 20 or so years. In 1991 about 37% of pensioners experienced poverty. This has fallen to about 14% – a significant decline. Pensioners' income has been protected by the government's decision to guarantee to increase the state pension every year by inflation or by a minimum of 2.5%. A very generous action compared to the 1% for those on other welfare benefits. The state pension and winter fuel allowance are still universal benefits. However critics argue it should be families that should be protected, not the elderly, and that the introduction of changes to the welfare system will increase child poverty.
(6 marks, range of knowledge, description/explanation, exemplification and extended analytical/ evaluative comment)

One aim of the Welfare State is to provide free comprehensive health care for all. The people of the UK do not pay to go to the doctors or worry about the cost of a hospital operation. With life expectancy increasing and deaths from cancer and heart attacks falling, it could be argued that the NHS is going some way to meeting its aims. In the last 25 years life expectancy has increased from 75 years to almost 80 years.

In recent years, the NHS has been protected from budget cuts and, despite long waiting lists and pressure on staff, it is still seen by many as 'the jewel in the crown' of the Welfare State. However, some argue that with an ageing population and greater expectations, the cost of delivering a 24–7 national service will become increasingly more difficult and the NHS will simply not be able to meet its original aims. Already, for example, there are differences between Scotland and England as pressure on the NHS mounts. Scotland is more collectivist and provides free prescriptions and eye tests and only uses the private sector to a limited extent. In contrast, prescription charges still exist in England. More importantly, the 2012 NHS England and Wales Act ends the need for the NHS to provide all services. This means that the private sector can bid to provide health services. So it could be argued that while the NHS in Scotland is still meeting its original aims, there are concerns that England is moving away from the original aims and principles of the NHS.
(8 marks, range of knowledge, description/explanation, exemplification and extended analytical/ evaluative comment

To conclude, the UK coalition government would argue that it is still meeting the core principles of the Welfare State – a comprehensive system that provides support from the cradle to the grave. However, the impact of massive public sector cuts is making it more difficult for the Welfare State to meet its aims. The different policies in England and Scotland over social and health care provision highlight the difference in priorities between the Scottish and UK governments.
(2 marks, overall evaluative comment that addresses the question)

Question		Detailed marking principles	Max mark
1.	(c)	**To what extent**	20

Credit responses that make reference to:

- Links between poverty and crime
- Analysis of other factors that cause criminal behaviour
- Balanced overall evaluative comment on the extent to which poverty is the main cause of criminal behaviour
- A clear, coherent line of argument

Credit reference to aspects of the following:

- Evidence of the link between poverty and criminal behaviour — most deprived regions experience significantly more crime/violent crime than affluent areas and more than half of Scotland's prison population have home addresses in the most deprived areas
- Evidence of the link between poverty and lack of educational attainment, high unemployment and mental health issues
- Other factors including biological factors ('criminal gene'), 'bad parenting', gender, alcohol and drugs, peer pressure/youth gangs, etc.
- Credit also criminological theories, e.g. positivists (crime caused by way people are and/or environment) and classical theories (crime is a choice/free will)

Any other valid point that meets the criteria described in the general marking principles for this kind of question.

Possible approaches to answering the question:

There is a clear link between poverty/deprivation and criminal behaviour. The Scottish Index of Multiple Deprivation (SIMD) shows that the most deprived areas experience more crime than other more affluent areas. For example, Glasgow, Renfrewshire and West Dunbartonshire have some of the highest levels of deprivation and as a result suffer the greatest levels of crime including violent crime.

(2 marks, accurate point with example)

Economic poverty impacts on educational attainment and stable family structures which, according to many criminologists such as Quetelet, are key factors in explaining criminal behaviour. Recent research suggests that about a third of prisoners have some form of learning disability while the same proportion have an IQ of 79 or less compared to an average among the wider population of 100. A deprived childhood can also lead to future criminal behaviour and in many cases there is a clear link to poverty. Over 20% of prisoners had been taken into care as a child. Adults taken into care when they were children make up 2% of the general public.

(4 marks, accurate point with explanation, exemplification and analysis)

As well as poverty, there are a great many other explanations as to why crime occurs. One explanation is so-called 'bad parenting'. This explanation talks about parents as poor role models who do not enforce boundaries as to what is right or wrong. They often have a poor attitude to authority and this too is passed on to their children. Government statistics show that an average of 43% of those in prison have had other family members in prison. Crime, it would appear, does run in families. Some criminologists go further with their analysis. They have argued that there is a 'criminal gene' which explains why many people from the same families end up in the criminal justice system. This is a classic 'nature' argument and there is some scientific evidence to support the view that certain individuals are predisposed to commit crime. However, most criminologists would not agree completely with this analysis and instead would argue that the nature of the individuals themselves is important but the surroundings in which they grow up is the key to criminality, i.e. 'nurture' is more important in influencing criminality.

(5 marks, accurate point with explanation, limited exemplification but extended analysis/ evaluative comment)

To conclude, evidence from the SIMD and prison statistics clearly indicate that poverty is one of the main causes, if not the main cause, of criminal behaviour. However, other factors such as alcohol and drug abuse, peer pressure and gender also play a part. Some types of crime, e.g. 'white collar crime', cannot be blamed on poverty but rather on greed. And how do we explain criminal behaviour, even murder, carried out by those from a comfortable and stable background? Does a criminal or 'evil gene' exist? The murder of teacher Ann Maguire by her student suggests that an 'evil gene' may exist. The murderer came from a good background and at his trial displayed no remorse for his actions.

(4 marks, overall evaluative conclusion that addresses the question)

Question		Detailed marking principles	Max mark
1.	(d)	**Discuss** **Credit responses that make reference to:** • Range of community-based punishments • Analysis of re-offending rates between prisons and community-based punishments • Balanced overall evaluative comment on the effectiveness of community-based punishments compared to prison • A clear, coherent line of argument **Credit reference to aspects of the following:** • Numbers re-offending after community-based punishments compared to those in prison. • Challenges experienced by prisons in ensuring prisoners are rehabilitated before release. Backdrop of overcrowding, too many prisoners on short sentences, lack of capacity within system to treat needs of individual prisoners, etc. • Relative strengths and weaknesses of alternative punishments such as Community Payback Order, Fiscal Disposal Orders (fines), home detention curfews , ASBOs, Drug Testing and Treatment Orders, restorative justice, etc. *Any other valid point that meets the criteria described in the general marking principles for this kind of question.* **Possible approaches to answering the question:** *Despite a fall in reported crime the Scottish (around 8,000 offenders in prison 2014) and UK prison population remains at a record high and this has a serious impact on the rehabilitation of criminals. Overcrowding stretches prison resources and reduces the opportunities for prisoners to take part in educational and offending-behaviour programmes. Too many offenders on short sentences and are in and out before their offending behaviour is addressed.* *(3 marks, accurate point with explanation, exemplification and analytical comment)* *In 2013, more than 1,000 offenders in Cambridgeshire were dealt with using restorative justice instead of more traditional methods of punishment. 51.9% of these cases involved young people and most instances were for minor offences. Restorative justice allows victims to help decide punishments for low-level crime, it provides an opportunity for offenders to understand the victims' pain and it can bring closure for those involved. Police said restorative justice had saved 8,000 policing hours and solved an extra 2.4% of crimes in the county in 2013. In Cambridgeshire, only 8% of those dealt with using restorative justice since April had committed further crimes. It would appear that for the police in Cambridgeshire restorative justice is far more effective in reducing re-offending than a prison sentence.* *(5 marks, accurate point, explanation, extended exemplification and analysis)* *Overall, there is substantial evidence to suggest that community-based punishments are more effective than prison both in terms of finance and especially in terms of reducing re-offending. This may be explained by the fact that community-based sentences can be arranged so that they better support the needs of the offender and challenge the offender to reflect on their behaviour. In addition, non-custodial sentences may allow offenders to continue to maintain their occupation, home and links with their family that can be lost through incarceration. These things are also important to reduce re-offending.* *(3 marks, conclusion with evaluative comment that addresses the question)*	20

Section 3 — International Issues

Question		Detailed marking principles	Max mark
1.		**Selectivity** **Examples of the types of evidence that support the view include:** • Source A: In 2012, Obama received almost 66 million votes, five million more than Romney. *(1 mark)* Link to Source C: Obama had 61.7% of the Electoral College vote and 51% of the popular vote. *(1 mark)* • Source A: Obama ... 'had huge support from a wide range of groups in society especially the young, poor groups and those from an ethnic minority background.' *(1 mark)* Backed up by Source B — young 60%, poorer (60% of up to $49,999), African-American 93%, Hispanic 71% and Asian 73%. *(1 mark)*	8

Question		Detailed marking principles	Max mark
1.		(continued)	
		Examples of types of evidence that does not support the view include:	
		• Source A: Romney '…won the popular vote in 24 of the 50 states and had narrow defeats in four states.' *(1 mark)* Link to Source C: Romney only 4% behind in popular vote (51% to 47.1%). *(1 mark)* • Source A stated: 'Romney's main support came from the old, the rich and white voters.' *(1 mark)* Backed up by Source B — Romney 56% of over 65 years, 53% of those earning over $200,000 and 59% of white voters. *(1 mark)*	
		Overall comment (Up to 2 marks available):	
		• The statement is only partially true. It could be argued (Source A) that it was outstanding for Obama to win over 60% of the Electoral College and in Source B to win the ethnic minority vote, especially over 90% of the African-American vote. *(1 mark)* • However, (Source C) Obama only won 51% of the popular votes and (Source B) more whites voted for Romney than for Obama, therefore it was not 'an outstanding victory for Obama'. *(1 mark)*	
		Comment/analysis on the origin or reliability of the source (Up to 2 marks available):	
		• On balance, the information is largely reliable. Information in Source A and C is taken from the BBC News website which has an international reputation of providing news in a fair and balanced way. Source B is information shared by the main television networks and is also seen as reliable. *(2 marks)* • Information in Source A is 'adapted' and this means that it may be subject to change or omission and therefore it may be less reliable than when originally written. *(1 mark)*	
		Any other relevant point.	
2.	(a)	**Analyse**	12
		Credit responses that make reference to:	
		• Ways in which a world power may exercise influence • An analysis of the influence of international involvement of a world power	
		Credit reference to aspects of the following — World Power: USA	
		• Leading member of NATO, biggest contributor — example of mobilising European action in the Ukraine crisis • Leading role in UN, P5 member of UN Security Council and biggest UN contributor • Military interventions — example of involvement in Afghanistan, Iraq and leading the fight against ISIS • Largest economy in the world and foremost military power; US Navy projects US military power around the globe • Role in Middle East and support for Israel • Member of G8 and G20	
		Any other valid point that meets the criteria described in the general marking principles for this kind of question.	
		Credit reference to aspects of the following — World Power: China	
		• Leading role as a permanent member of UN Security Council • Vetoed the intervention of Western powers in Darfur and Syria • Member of the BRICS countries — Brazil, Russia, India, China and South Africa • Investment in African countries and elsewhere • Growing influence in South-East Asia and has territorial disputes with neighbouring countries, Japan, Vietnam and India • Issue of Taiwan creates tension with the USA • Growing importance of China in world economy (close second to the USA)	
		Any other valid point that meets the criteria described in the general marking principles for this kind of question.	
		Possible approaches to answering the question — World Power: China	
		The USA role, as the only superpower, ensures that its international involvement and influence covers the entire globe with involvement that covers Europe, Africa, Asia and South America. ***(1 mark, accurate and exemplified but underdeveloped point)***	

Question		Detailed marking principles	Max mark
2.	(a)	**(continued)** *The USA is an extremely influential world power with the world's largest economy and unrivalled military strength. The US is the only military superpower. In recent years the US has spent more on defence than the next nine nations combined, although the US is having to cut back on defence spending as it can now longer afford to spend as much.* *The US dominates NATO, although all members are supposedly equal, and it has used its influence to ensure that NATO played its part in Afghanistan. During the Afghan War the US contributed by far the most hardware and troops with over 100,000 US soldiers in the country a few years back. Most commentators would agree that NATO needs the US but the US does not always need NATO.* **(4 marks, two relevant points each with some explanation, exemplification and analysis)** *The USA has huge influence in the Western Pacific and the Far East, with bases in places such as the Philippines, but is facing a growing challenge from China. For example, the USA supports Taiwan, which the Chinese government regards as being part of China, and this creates tension between the two countries. The Americans provide Taiwan with up-to-date military hardware and this sends a clear message to China that the US intends that Taiwan should not rejoin China. The US also backs Japan the traditional Chinese rival in the Far East.* *The rapid growth of China's economy and military might — China is building its first aircraft carrier — makes it difficult for the USA to main the same level of influence as it did in the past. However, the USA still dominates the seas as it has 10 aircraft carriers, four based in the Pacific. The USA also retains troops in Japan and South Korea and so the USA still dominates the region. The USA is closely watching China's aggressive territorial claims against its neighbours, especially Japan. In recent years it has been claimed that the US has been working harder to maintain its influence in the Far East than in Europe and this may explain why Russia has been able to get away with annexing the Crimea. It may also show US influence is not all that it once was.* **(7 marks, accurate developed series of points with description, explanation, exemplification and extended analysis)**	
	(b)	**Analyse** **Credit responses that make reference to:** • Relevant socio-economic issues • Analysis of the ways the government has sought to tackle these **Credit reference to aspects of the following — World Power: USA** • Housing vouchers — government pays 70% of rent • Child Care and Development Fund — Temporary Assistance for Needy Families extra money to pay for childcare • Food stamps (Supplemental Nutrition Assistance Programme) — can be exchanged for food • Earned Income Tax Credit (tax reduction) and 'Welfare to Work' • Medicaid/Medicare — Free Health Care Social/Health Patient Protection and Affordable Care Act (2010) — more Americans have affordable/quality health care • Head Start — same as hungry for success in the UK — healthier school meals/more PE, health, etc. • Affirmative Action as it operates today • The American Recovery and Reinvestment Act (2012) • Race to the Top — Equity and Opportunity (2014) *Any other valid point that meets the criteria described in the general marking principles for this kind of question.* **Credit reference to aspects of the following — World Power: China** • China has developed a 'socialist market economy' over the past 30 years. China has second largest economy (may pass soon) after USA with increases of around 9.5% per annum. • China's GDP has increased from just over $200 billion in 1980 to $9.2 trillion in 2014. • Gap between rich and poor, urban and rural has widened. Inequality issue of concern to CPC. • Issue of migrant workers in terms of housing, social services and education for their families. • Inequalities have widened with Gini index increasing to 0.47, passing the USA's 0.40, which is seen as high.	12

Question		Detailed marking principles	Max mark
2.	(b)	**(continued)** • Numerous government programmes to reduce poverty being developed including basis for a social security system, poverty alleviation, Free Lunch for Children programme, etc. • Investment to expand access to health care and education • There have been huge improvements in the standard of living for the majority although millions continue to experience poverty including many in the countryside and migrant workers, e.g. average urban disposable incomes are three times that of the average rural disposable income. *Any other valid point that meets the criteria described in the general marking principles for this kind of question.* **Possible approaches to answering the question — World Power: USA** *One government policy to tackle economic inequality is the Supplemental Nutrition Assistance Programme. This is known as Food Stamps and about 45 million people, one in seven Americans, buy food with it. However for a single person it is only 30 dollars' worth of groceries for a week.* ***(2 marks, accurate point with explanation)*** *President Obama has pushed through the Affordable Care Act which aims to provide every American with some form of affordable basic health insurance. The USA does not have a free NHS like the UK. 'Obamacare', as it is known, has widened access to US government health care or brought in subsidies to reduce the cost of private medical care. All US citizens must now have some form of health care or face a fine. Many cannot afford this or are rejected for insurance because of health issues. This has been made illegal and explains why 15% of the American public had no cover before the Act.* ***(4 marks, accurate point with extended explanation, exemplification and analysis)*** *Recent government health reforms are attempting to reduce health inequalities by aiming to provide every American with affordable basic health insurance. In 2012, 48 million Americans were uninsured, 15% of the American public. The Affordable Care Act ('Obamacare') makes it illegal for insurance companies to deny health coverage to the ill or to charge them more than healthy or young people. The Act requires all Americans to obtain insurance or face a fine. One consequence of the Affordable Care Act is that wealthy Americans will have to pay more for health cover and this is why the Republicans (most support from wealthy) oppose 'Obamacare'. The Act also expands Medicare, which is the public health programme for the poor, and offers subsidies to help low earners buy private health care. This policy helps the poor and ethnic minorities and so far an extra 9 million Americans now have health care. Although there is a second court challenge to the Affordable Care Act, it has already helped thousands of Americans gain health treatment.* ***(7 marks, accurate developed point with description explanation, exemplification and extended analysis)***	
	(c)	**Analyse** **Credit responses that make reference to:** • Background to a world issue • Analysis of the actions taken by international organisations to resolve an issue **Credit reference to aspects of the following:** • World issue: International terrorism (UN/NATO) • World issue: Developing world poverty (UN agencies/NGOs) • World issue: Nuclear proliferation (UN) • World issue: Global economic crisis (EU/World Bank/IMF) *Any other valid point that meets the criteria described in the general marking principles for this kind of question.* **Possible approaches to answering the question:** *NATO plays an important role in the war against international terrorism. Intelligence cooperation led to the establishment of the Terrorist Threat Intelligence Unit at NATO headquarters in Brussels. This allows countries to share information and consult one another on suspected terrorists and possible plots, e.g. information gathered about weapons of mass destruction, and was used in the fight against the Taliban and Al-Qaeda in Afghanistan.* ***(3 marks, accurate point with explanation and exemplification)***	12

Question		Detailed marking principles	Max mark
2.	(c)	**(continued)**	
		Development in Africa can be undermined by the impact of infectious diseases such as HIV/AIDS and more recently the Ebola crisis. Ebola is a viral illness which has broken out in Liberia, Sierra Leone and Guinea, three of the world's poorest countries. Liberia has only 620 beds but needs five times that number to treat the numbers infected. UN specialised agencies, such as WHO, are working hard to contain the disease that has killed over 5,000 people. The WHO has deployed teams of experts to West African countries including epidemiologists to work with countries in surveillance and medical experts to supply mobile field labs for early confirmation of Ebola cases. WHO and other organisations are working on instant diagnosis kits which will enable health care workers to isolate patients early when the disease is hard to tell from malaria or cholera. The WHO has set health guidelines and goals: 70% of burials must be safe and 70% of cases isolated. The World Bank and EU countries have pledged $2 million — a 70-bed clinic costs $1 million a month to run and needs two staff for each patient. WHO has been praised for its decisive actions which has prevented the disease spreading across Nigeria and Senegal and each country has reported no further cases. ***(7 marks, accurate developed point with description, extended explanation and exemplification and detailed analysis)***	
	(d)	**Analyse**	12
		Credit responses that make reference to: • Background to a world issue • Analysis of its impact on those affected **Credit reference to aspects of the following:** • War/conflict — Afghanistan, Libya, Syria, Ukraine, Middle East, etc. • Nuclear weapons — North Korea • Economic difficulties — EU countries (Portugal, Ireland, Italy, Greece, Spain) • Development issues in Africa • Crisis in Eastern Europe *Any other valid point that meets the criteria described in the general marking principles for this kind of question.* **Possible approaches to answering the question:** *Ukraine was once part of the Soviet Union but became an independent country after the collapse of communism in 1991. The current Russian leader, Putin, is determined to prevent Ukraine from becoming part of NATO. Russia has armed pro-Russian groups in Eastern Ukraine and has taken control of Crimea and it now is part of Russia.* ***(2 marks, accurate point with development)*** *Russia's attempt to restore its influence in parts of its former empire has had serious and deadly consequences for the people of Ukraine. Russia has armed pro-Russian groups in Eastern Ukraine who have rebelled against the Ukrainian government in Kiev. Around 4,000 citizens and soldiers have died in the conflict and many are missing or held hostage by the rebels. Many Ukrainians have lost their homes and have had to flee to Western Ukraine to escape from the fighting. The Ukrainian people in Crimea, now annexed by Russia, have effectively lost their nationality. In the near future there is little hope of peace. Despite attempts at ceasefires and peace talks, both sides seem as far apart as ever. The movement of Russian troops and armour into Eastern Ukraine has increased the chances of the war widening.* ***(5 marks, accurate developed point with explanation, exemplification and analysis)*** *For the people of Russia the consequences of the crisis in Ukraine are mixed. The media is completely controlled by the government and the public are said to largely believe the propaganda that the Ukrainian government is illegal and fascist and that it is persecuting the pro-Russian Ukrainians. They have been told that Crimea has returned to the 'motherland' and that Putin is only supplying humanitarian aid to the Donetsk region. It is reported that they feel no shame over the downing of the Boeing plane and the 297 innocents who died, claiming it was Ukrainian troops who shot the plane down.* *However, the economic sanctions imposed by the West as a response have had some impact. For example, Russian business has been squeezed and the rouble has lot a great deal of its international currency value. Also, it is clear that many Russian soldiers have lost their lives in the conflict in Ukraine. The Russian media reports that these soldiers took leave to go and fight with their pro-Russian Ukrainian colleagues. Russia denies they were ordered into the war zone by their commanders.* ***(7 marks, accurate developed point with explanation, exemplification and extended analysis)***	

HIGHER FOR CfE MODERN STUDIES
MODEL PAPER 3

Section 1 — Democracy in Scotland and UK

Question		Detailed marking principles	Max mark
1.	(a)	**Discuss** **Credit responses that make reference to:** • The main features of an electoral system or systems • Analysis of the ways the electoral system or systems provide fair or unfair representation • Balanced overall evaluative comment on the extent to which the electoral system or systems provide fair representation • A clear, coherent line of argument **Credit reference to aspects of the following (UK Dimension):** **First Past The Post (FPTP) (Elections to the UK Parliament)** • Straightforward/decisive: candidate with the greatest number of votes becomes the MP; party with the most MPs forms the government • Direct representation between MP and voters which increases accountability • Usually produces majority government with the winning party having the opportunity to implement its manifesto promises • Usually avoids coalition government with compromise politics **Balanced by:** • Candidates often win on minority of vote • Votes do not reflect seats gained as some parties remain under-represented compared to their share of national vote • Tends to exaggerate seats of Conservative and Labour and produce a two-party system; encourages tactical voting • Argument that FPTP promotes voter apathy as 'safe seats' ensure one party's dominance. Many voters therefore, consider their vote a 'wasted vote'. **Credit reference to aspects of the following (Scottish dimension):** **Additional Member System (AMS) (Elections to the Scottish Parliament)** • Greater degree of proportionality which usually ensures wider range of parties represented in Scottish Parliament • Argument that a greater proportion of voters get some of the policies that they voted for • Provides direct constituency representation and national proportionality • Arguably, there is greater opportunity to choose and elect female or ethnic-minority candidates **Balanced by:** • Two sets of representatives (constituency and list) can be confusing for voters • Parties control lists • Greater likelihood of minority or coalition government with compromise politics • Not as proportional as some other forms of PR **Single Transferable Vote (STV) (Scottish local government elections)** • Highly proportional • No need for tactical voting • Voters can choose within and between parties; multi-member wards provide choice of representatives to contact • Arguably, there is greater opportunity to choose and elect female or ethnic-minority candidates **Balanced by:** • More likely to result in coalition politics with compromise politics • More complex than other electoral systems which it could be argued confuses or puts off electors from voting; there may be confusion over which representative to contact • Difficult to replace representatives who resign *Any other valid point that meets the criteria described in the general marking principles for this type of question*	20

Question		Detailed marking principles	Max mark
1.	(a)	**(continued)**	
		Possible approaches to answering the question:	
		When FPTP is used voters make a clear choice of the most popular candidate. Many would argue this is fair. Some other electoral systems, e.g. AMS, do not allow all the representatives to be directly chosen by voters. With their second vote, electors choose a party and those at the top of the party list would be elected.	
		(2 marks, accurate point with explanation and analytical comment)	
		Under FPTP, used for elections to the UK Parliament, a party can form the government when another party has won more votes nationally. This happens because governments are formed on the basis of how many seats a party wins and not the number of votes it secures from all UK voters. At constituency level, a candidate may also win with a minority of the vote. In some constituencies an MP may be elected with a minority of the vote, e.g. Malcolm Bruce MP in Gordon elected on a 36% share of the vote in 2010.	
		(3 marks, accurate point with explanation, exemplification and analytical comment)	
		AMS could be said to be fairer than other systems such as FPTP or STV. With AMS, electors get two votes — one for a constituency MSP and one for a regional list MSP. The constituency vote (there are 73 constituency MSPs) is fair because, as with FPTP, the candidate with the most support wins. In Dundee West in 2011 this was Joe Fitzpatrick. The second vote, for a party on a regional list, helps to bring proportionality to the result. For example, the Conservatives and Labour returned no MSPs in the North East Scotland constituency vote in 2011 but they were given two and three MSPs on the list vote to make the overall result in NE Scotland fairer. However, AMS is not completely fair as other systems such as STV are more proportional that AMS. As parties control the regional lists, it could be argued that this is not fair either.	
		(5 marks, accurate point with explanation, exemplification and analysis)	
		To conclude, AMS would appear to be fairer than FPTP both in terms of proportionality and in terms of representing more accurately the choices of voters. It may also be said that voters get the best of both worlds with proportionality and a directly-elected constituency MSP. Equally, it could be argued that STV is fairer still because it is more proportional than AMS, all votes count and constituents can choose within and between representatives. Parties also control the regional list, not voters. FPTP would appear to be the least fair as at both constituency level and national level candidates or parties can win on a minority of the vote. FPTP has strengths but 'fairness' would not appear to be one of them.	
		(4 marks, balanced overall comment with well-argued conclusion)	
	(b)	**To what extent**	20
		Credit responses that make reference to: • Range of pressure groups and ways in which pressure groups attempt to influence government • Analysis of the ways pressure groups influence decision-making in government • Balanced overall evaluative comment on the extent of pressure-group influence on decision-making in government • A clear, coherent line of argument	
		Credit reference to aspects of the following: • Cause or interest groups can promote a single issue, e.g. nuclear disarmament, or represent sectional interests, e.g. trade unions, National Farmers' Union, etc. Groups with financial means and larger membership and with a cause that has government support likely to be more successful. • Insider and outsider groups. Insider groups such as BMA have excellent ties with government decision-makers and are often included in private discussions. Outsider groups lack official recognition and have to convert/mobilise public opinion or take action to assert influence, e.g. students protesting against the raising of student fees used marches, petitions, demonstrations, media campaigns, etc. • Examples of successful action includes the Scottish legal profession persuading the Scottish government to delay the repeal of corroboration in Scottish court cases. Also, the Gurkhas winning rights to stay in the UK. • Examples of failed pressure-group activity include groups campaigning for an elected UK second chamber not achieving the promised reform as a Conservative backbench revolt led to the House of Lords Reform Bill being dropped.	
		Any other valid point that meets the criteria described in the general marking principles	
		Possible approaches to answering the question:	
		The methods that a pressure group uses will depend on its relationship with the government. If it is respected and has significant influence it may work directly with the government. The BMA is an example of an insider group and promoted the banning of smoking in public places	
		(2 marks, accurate point with an example)	

Question		Detailed marking principles	Max mark

1.	(b)	**(continued)**
		
		The methods that a pressure group uses (lobbying, marches and demonstrations, media campaigns, etc.) may depend on its relationship with the government. If it is respected and it shares the same ideas and principles as the government then it is more likely to be listened to and have influence. The BMA is an example of an insider group which has campaigned strongly to restrict the use of tobacco use and tobacco advertising. The BMA has, on occasion, been invited to give expert advice directly to government ministers when the government is looking to pass legislation. Although it is difficult to work out the extent to which insider groups influence government (most of the work of insider groups is not undertaken in public) there is no doubt the BMA has been successful to an extent as tobacco advertising has been restricted and there is a ban on smoking in enclosed public places throughout the UK.
		   (5 marks, accurate point with explanation, exemplification and extended analytical comment)
		
		The methods that a pressure group uses (lobbying, marches and demonstrations, media campaigns, etc.) may depend on its relationship with the government. If it is respected and it shares the same ideas and principles as the government then it is more likely to be listened to and have influence.
		
		The BMA is an example of an insider group which, on occasion, has been invited to give expert advice directly to government ministers when the government is looking to pass legislation. For example, the SNP government consulted with the BMA and received its support over the introduction of free prescriptions. It has provided guidance to the Scottish and UK governments on diet, exercise and safe alcohol consumption. Also, in both Scotland and England/Wales, the BMA has campaigned against tobacco use and tobacco advertising. Although it is difficult to work out the extent to which insider groups influence government (most of the work of insider groups is not undertaken in public) there is no doubt the BMA has been successful to an extent as tobacco advertising has been restricted and there is a ban on smoking in enclosed public places throughout the UK.
		
		Outsider groups are treated differently to insider groups. They are unlikely to be consulted by the government over policy and legislation and have little direct contact with the government. These outsider groups try to mobilise public opinion and achieve media attention through publicity campaigns. The Campaign for Nuclear Disarmament (CND) has been trying to get rid of nuclear weapons for over 50 years but with no success.
		   (8 marks, range of knowledge, description/explanation, exemplification and extended analytical comment)
		
		Overall, it can be difficult to assess the effectiveness of pressure groups in influencing government decision-making. It is clear that insider groups often work in partnership with government, making a judgement on the extent of their influence very difficult. However, insider groups are not always successful in achieving all their aims. For example, while the BMA supports the introduction of free prescriptions across the UK, the coalition government has not introduced free prescriptions in England. On the other hand, the success of the high-profile Gurkha Justice Campaign, which received a great deal of media publicity and massive public support, illustrates the power of united public opinion. The Labour UK government was forced to back down and allow all Gurkhas who had served in the British army prior to 1997 residency and welfare rights. So although insider groups appear to have more influence, outsider groups may also influence government in certain circumstances.
		   (4 marks, balanced overall comment with well-argued conclusion)	

Section 2 — Social Issues in the UK

Question		Detailed marking principles	Max mark
1.		**Selectivity** **The extent to which Stop and Search is used in different parts of the world** The use of Stop and Search in Scotland is rising and much higher in Scotland but less/falling in England and New York City. • Source A states that the use of Stop and Search has 'widened' in Scotland with Fife demonstrating a 400% increase year-on-year. *(1 mark)* Source A also states that in England Stop and Search has decreased by 15% and in NYC fewer people have been stopped and searched since 2013. *(1 mark)* • Source B shows Scotland has a Stop and Search rate of 970 per 10,000 people compared to England at 330 and NYC at 110 per 10,000 people. *(1 mark)* **(Max. 3 marks)**	8

Question		Detailed marking principles	Max mark
1.		**(continued)** **The use of Stop and Search on different groups** Those who are searched the most are the young (under 20 years) and those from minority groups. • Source A states Stop and Search rates in Scotland are greatest amongst younger people with 500 children aged 10 years and under stopped and searched in 2010. *(1 mark)* Source C shows that 83% of those aged 14 and under and 78% of those aged 15–20 were non-statutory stops, the highest of all the age groups given. *(1 mark)* • Source A states: 'Of the 612,110 stop and searches by police officers in the Strathclyde area in 2012/13, 55.2% were carried out on the 16 to 29 age group.' *(1 mark)* • Source A states: 'In 2013, the Equality and Human Rights Commission (EHRC) said in some parts of England black people were 29 times more likely to be stopped and searched.' *(1 mark)* Source A also states that in New York 'More of those stopped and frisked were black and Hispanic.' *(1 mark)* *(Max. 3 marks)* **Possible overall conclusions:** *Overall, it would appear that Scotland is going in the opposite direction with Stop and Search compared to England and NYC. Scotland's rate of Stop and Search is increasing while the rate of use in England and NYC is falling. (1 mark)* *Overall, it would appear that Scotland is going in the opposite direction with Stop and Search compared to England and NYC. Our rate of Stop and Search is increasing while the rate of use in England and NYC is falling. In addition, Stop and Search would appear to disproportionately affect young people and those from an ethnic-minority background. This is true of all three areas mentioned in the sources. (2 marks)* • Any other relevant point	
2.	(a)	**Analyse** **Credit responses that make reference to:** • Evidence of social inequality in Scottish or UK society • Analysis of the causes of inequalities **Credit reference to aspects of the following:** • Evidence of inequalities in terms of income, wealth, health and life expectancy, gender, ethnicity, education, housing, etc. • Range of views as to the causes of inequalities including impact of poverty and deprivation, lifestyle choices, hereditary factors, discrimination in its many forms, lack of social mobility, government policy, etc. • Credit also sociological perspectives, e.g. those on the political left blame poverty, discrimination, government policy, etc. whereas those on the right claim society better rewards the most able (natural order) and hardest working (lack of individual responsibility, etc.) *Any other valid point that meets the criteria described in the general marking principles for this type of question.* **Possible approaches to answering the question:** *Research from the Resolution Foundation shows that many people in work live below the poverty line. Low wages, an insufficient National Minimum Wage (only £6.50 per hour for an adult) and zero-hour contracts means that millions of people are 'working poor'.* <div align="right">*(2 marks, accurate point with an example)*</div> *Many elderly people experience social inequality, especially those who depend totally on their State Pension (only £113.10 per week for a single pensioner). Although the poorest elderly people can top up their benefits with Pension Credit and are entitled to heating allowances (Cold Weather Payments and Winter Fuel Payment), many still struggle. A few people blame elderly people for their poverty, saying they should have saved harder or looked for better employment when of working age. However, most people would argue that low wages earlier in their lives meant that many people couldn't afford to save for their retirement and that Social Security payments in retirement are not enough to provide for an adequate standard of living.* <div align="right">*(4 marks, accurate point, with explanation, exemplification and analytical comment)*</div>	12

Question		Detailed marking principles	Max mark
2.	(a)	**(continued)**	
		Gender inequality is one type of social inequality. Some people say that gender stereotyping is a cause of social inequality. The expectation among many employers and some people in wider society is that women should take responsibility for housework and for childcare. This view reduces the chances of women gaining better-paid employment. Also, as nine out of ten lone parents are women, this too may prevent women from accessing well-paid employment and extending their careers. It is said women are often concentrated in the 5 Cs such as catering or cleaning where wages are traditionally lower.	
		Women are also said to hit the 'glass ceiling' which is an invisible barrier that prevents women achieving the highest levels in their career. Recently, there has been a number of women who have taken their employer to court under the Equality Act of 2010.	
		Finally, the impact of the recession has affected women more than men. The Fawcett Society highlights that since 2010 three times as many women as men have lost their jobs in the public sector.	
		(6 marks, range of points with description, explanation and analytical comment)	
	(b)	**Analyse**	12
		Credit responses that make reference to:	
		• Government policies to tackle wealth inequalities	
		• Analysis of way in which different policies are expected to operate	
		Credit reference to aspects of the following:	
		• Wide range of welfare provision including state benefits, health care, education, housing and children's social services	
		• Reforms to the Welfare State (including introduction of Universal Credit, cap on benefit limits, etc.) and reasons behind reforms, e.g. to 'make work pay', target 'deserving poor', etc.	
		• Raising of income tax threshold to take lowest paid out of income tax altogether	
		• Promise by many local councils to adopt 'living wage'	
		• Scottish dimension — retention of universal benefits including continuation of free personal care, measures to support those affected by the 'bedroom tax', etc.	
		• Credit view that those on the right of politics do not make it a policy to reduce income or wealth inequalities, e.g. reduction in top-rate income tax	
		Any other valid point that meets the criteria described in the general marking principles for this type of question.	
		Possible approaches to answering the question:	
		The Employability, Skills and Lifelong Learning budget received additional funding of £6 million in 2013–14 and 2014–15 as part of an overall package of £30 million to support the implementation of 'Opportunities for All'. This programme aims to reduce social inequality in Scotland.	
		(1 mark, one relevant point explained)	
		Work Programmes were launched in 2011. They replaced New Deal. People claiming Universal Credit can now be referred instantly to a WP and do not have to wait six months. WPs are designed to be 'tough on the job-shy but supportive of the job-ready'. The quicker referral period will enable unemployed people to more readily obtain work.	
		(2 marks, accurate point with evaluative comment)	
		The coalition government at Westminster has introduced a number of changes to tackle poverty in the UK. For example, Universal Credit (UC) was introduced in 2013. UC replaces a wide range of benefits, such as Jobseeker's Allowance, Employment Support Allowance and Housing Benefit. According to the government, the aims of Universal Credit are to simplify the benefits system and bring together a range of working-age benefits into a single payment to better support those in need. Supporters of the coalition government's changes hope they will reduce 'in-work poverty' and 'make work pay' although the Conservatives do not state reducing inequality as an aim. However, those who oppose the coalition claim UC and other reforms of the Social Security system, such as the so-called 'bedroom tax', have led to a reduced income for many of the poorest people. This, it is claimed, has widened social inequality.	
		(5 marks, accurate and developed point, exemplified, with analytical comment)	

Question		Detailed marking principles	Max mark
2.	(c)	**Analyse**	12
		Credit responses that make reference to:	
		• Policies of the police to tackle crime • Analysis of the way in which different policies are expected to operate	
		Credit reference to aspects of the following:	
		• Community-based policing and its aims • Proactive policing, e.g. Stop and Search, high-visibility policing in areas with high crime rates or where there are many repeat offenders, etc. and aims of these policies • Debate over proactive policing and reactive policing • Serious Organised Crime Task Force and Serious Organised Crime Strategy; establishing of Scottish Crime Campus • Introduction of Police Scotland to allow greater cooperation and sharing of resources across the country and to better network with other countries • Credit differences in approach between Scotland and rest of the UK where accurate and relevant	
		Any other valid point that meets the criteria described in the general marking principles for this type of question.	
		Possible approaches to answering the question:	
		One police policy is to work with local areas through community policing. Police officers are assigned to an area to work with community groups to understand the needs of the community and to build better relations. Police aim to be 'citizens in uniform' and not to be regarded as 'the enemy'.	
		<div align="center">**(2 marks, accurate point with explanation, and analytical comment)**</div>	
		One police policy is to work with local areas through community policing. Police officers are assigned to an area to work with community groups to understand the needs of the community and to build better relations. Police aim to be 'citizens in uniform' and not to be regarded as 'the enemy'.	
		As part of community policing, across Scotland over 50 officers work with secondary schools as 'campus cops'. Officers build up relations with young people and give talks on antisocial behaviour, drugs and the danger of carrying knives. Through a range of learning activities, the police can improve their knowledge of the community and help identify young people at risk of involvement in crime or gang-related violence. This policy, it has been said, has helped to reduce youth crime, including knife crime, in Scotland.	
		<div align="center">**(5 marks, accurate point with explanation, exemplification and analytical comment)**</div>	
	(d)	**Analyse**	12
		Credit responses that make reference to:	
		• Criminal behaviour and links to social factors • Alternative views to explain criminal behaviour	
		Credit reference to aspects of the following:	
		• Statistical correlation between the most deprived areas of Scotland or the UK and highest crime rates, greatest number of offenders, etc. • Criminological explanations of links between individual/community poverty and crime, e.g. sociological positivism, 'nurture' arguments, etc. • Impact of other social factors including gender, age and ethnicity on crime levels • Alternative views to explain crime, e.g. Classical School, 'nature' arguments, etc.	
		Any other valid point that meets the criteria described in the general marking principles for this type of question.	
		Possible approaches to answering the question:	
		Official statistics suggest crime is linked to age. Middle-aged and elderly people have far lower arrest and conviction rates than people in their 20s and 30s. For example, according to the Scottish Offenders Index the peak age for offending in Scotland in 2013 was 23 years for men and 30 for women.	
		<div align="center">**(2 marks, relevant point with an example)**</div>	

Question		Detailed marking principles	Max mark
2.	(d)	**(continued)** *Poverty, is has long been recognised, is key cause of crime. Statistics from the Scottish government year-on-year show that those arrested or found guilty in court are more likely to live in the most deprived parts of the country. Although more affluent people do commit crime and in the London riots in 2011 some of those arrested were professional, working people, proportionally more crime is carried out by poorer people. However, this is not to say that all poor people commit crime, far from it. The vast majority of people, including those classed as poor, are honest and obey the law.* *(3 marks, accurate point with extended analytical comment)* *Gender plays an important part in causing criminal behaviour. For example, in 2014 the Scottish Prison Service held 7,731 prisoners of whom only around 500 were female. Also, in the UK, men were reported as more likely to commit crime than women and a significantly greater number of men have been sentenced to life imprisonment, e.g. 364 out of 384 life imprisonment sentences have been given to men. In Scotland in 2012, official figures show that 79% of all violent crime was carried out by men.* *There are different views to explain why more men are involved in crime. Some criminologists, including Sutherland (1949), would argue that society more strictly controls girls and that there are clear societal roles for girls and roles for boys. These roles, he argued, encourage boys to take risks and to be tough and aggressive and this partly explains higher male crime rates especially for violence. Other criminologists, such as Carlen (1990), have argued that women turn to crime only when in a male-dominated society women have little or no other choice. This may partly explain why the majority of female crime is non-violent.* *(6 marks, range of knowledge, explanation, exemplification and extended analytical comment)*	

Section 3 — International Issues

Question	Detailed marking principles	Max mark
1.	**Selectivity** **Examples of the types of evidence that support the view include:** • Source A states: 'In 2009, a majority of the US public registered approval of Obama's foreign policy, far ahead of the figure achieved by recent US presidents.' Source B supports this as Obama's foreign policy approval rate rose from about 40% to 58% in the first half of 2009. *(2 marks)* • Source A states: 'In May 2011 Bin Laden was eliminated in Pakistan and a further 30 top leaders were killed by drone attacks.' Source B supports this as Obama's foreign policy approval rate rose from about 46% in late 2008 to 58% in the first half of 2009. *(2 marks)* **Examples of types of evidence that does not support the view include:** • Source A states: 'However, with the early failure to locate and capture Bin Laden, the American public became less supportive of Obama's foreign policy.' This is supported by Source B which highlights that Obama's overall approval rate fell from around 70% in 2009 to under 50% in 2010. *(2 marks)* • Source A states: 'Libya was a failure' and '(ISIS or Islamic State) is regarded as a major security threat to the area and the US'. Source B supports this as it shows that Obama's foreign policy approval rate fell again from 50% in January 2013 to a then all-time low of 35% in the middle of 2013. *(2 marks)* **Overall comment** (Up to 2 marks available): The statement 'President Obama's foreign policy is popular with the US public' has become, in the main, less true since the middle of 2009. *(1 mark)* It would also appear to be the case that over Obama's presidency most of his foreign policy actions, e.g. Libya and Syria, have resulted in a drop in public support for the president. *(1 mark)* **Comment/analysis on the origin or reliability of the source** (Up to 2 marks available): Information in Source A is taken from a variety of news articles which are not dated or referenced. It has also been adapted. This makes Source A very unreliable. *(1 mark)* Source B is from 'Huffpollster' and it is stated that this is a respected US polling agency. This source is likely to be more reliable although no date is given for this source. These sources should be used with care. *(1 mark)* Any other relevant point.	8

Question		Detailed marking principles	Max mark

2.	(a)	**Evaluate**
		
		Credit responses that make reference to:
		• The political system in the world power
		• Evaluative comment on the extent to which the political system is democratic
		
		Credit reference to aspects of the following — World Power: China
		• Chinese leaders, including Xi, have repeatedly claimed they have no desire to introduce 'western-style democracy'. Outside Hong Kong there is no mass pro-democracy movement. Democracy is a largely alien concept to China, a country which is used to power being centralised.
		• The leading role of the CPC is written into the Chinese constitution. Xi aims to see the CPC lead the 'rejuvenation' of China.
		• Although there are other political parties they are not in opposition to the CPC .
		• Close control of the media and limits to internet access
		• Despite regional pressure there is no political autonomy for minorities in, for example, Tibet or Xinjiang.
		• At town and village level Chinese citizens can choose their representatives. There are nominally 'independent' candidates. However, the CPC oversees all elections and keeps a close eye on those elected.
		• CPC tolerates some limited criticism from academics and general public, but only then in government-controlled forums, e.g. opinion polls and focus groups ('deliberative democracy'). Widespread political protest in Hong Kong although CPC slowly re-exerting control.
		• Most groups and individuals are still unable to obtain government permission to publish work if it contradicts CPC rhetoric. These private publishers are subject to the threat of closure and arrest each time they exercise their right to freedom of expression.
		
		Any other valid point that meets the criteria described in the general marking principles for this type of question.
		
		Credit reference to aspects of the following — World Power: USA
		• USA has a written constitution which protects the rights of its citizens
		• The US constitution divides powers between the federal government (foreign affairs, currency, etc.) and states (everything that is not given to the federal government).
		• The democratic system is based on the 'separation of powers' between the Executive (Presidency), Legislative (Congress) and Judiciary (Supreme Court). A similar model applies at state level.
		• Congress consists of two houses — the Senate (100 Senators, two from each state) and the House of Representatives (435 Congressmen/women). Congress has the sole right to legislate.
		• President is elected through an electoral college. President has number of defined powers but these are limited in range of ways by Congress. Congress can impeach the president if he oversteps powers.
		• US has a free media with free opportunity to join pressure groups and to protest against government actions.
		• Numerous elections at all levels to ensure government accountability.
		• Criticism of US political system in that wealthy elite dominate.
		• Criticism that new voting rules, e.g. requirement to have photo ID to vote in Texas, are preventing poorest groups of Americans from voting.
		
		Any other valid point that meets the criteria described in the general marking principles for this type of question.
		
		Possible approaches to answering the question — World Power: China
		
		The CPC leadership has accepted that there must be some controlled political reform ('democracy with Chinese characteristics') to keep the CPC in power and to improve the efficiency of China and its government.
		        (1 mark, accurate point with explanation)
		
		The CPC leadership (Hu and Xi) have claimed that China will never adopt 'western-style democracy'. The leadership believe than any attempt to introduce free elections would be detrimental to China both economically and socially. Instead, the CPC aims to make itself more receptive to public opinion by seeking to develop practices that allow it to listen to the demands of the people and to react more appropriately, e.g. increased use of public opinion polls or through the use of focus groups. One commentator has called this approach developing a 'deliberative democracy'.
		        (3 marks, accurate point with explanation, exemplification and analytical comment)
			12

Question		Detailed marking principles	Max mark
2.	**(a)**	**(continued)**	
		'Grassroots democracy' or democracy from the 'bottom up' has been developing in China for several years. The first direct elections were held in rural villages in 1988 and by the early 1990s a law was introduced which established elections in every village across the country. More recently, at the next level up, there have been elections in some of the townships. Although generally democratic in nature, the way in which elections and local government operate is not quite the same as in most democracies. Firstly, the elections are overseen by the CPC with most candidates needing prior CPC approval. Secondly, once elected, town and village committees often find their powers limited by local CPC officials. 'Independent candidates' who protest about their lack of decision-making power may be prevented from standing for re-election.	
		(4 marks, accurate point with explanation, exemplification and extended analytical comment)	
		Overall, the Chinese cannot claim their political system to be democratic when compared to the West. Despite the fact that change has occurred, e.g. 'deliberative democracy', power still lies firmly with the CPC. The dominant position of the CPC is written into the Chinese constitution and this is not up for discussion. China will remain a one-party state. Democracy also requires multi-party politics, it requires free association and a free media. These things are not available in China.	
		(3 marks, overall evaluate comment that addresses the question)	
	(b)	**Evaluate**	**12**
		Credit reference to aspects of the following:	
		• Social and economic issues • Evaluation of the effectiveness of the government tackling relevant social and economic issues	
		Credit reference to aspects of the following — World Power: China	
		• Relevant social/economic issues may include inequality, unemployment/under-employment, environmental pollution, crime, etc. • China has developed a 'socialist market economy' over the past 30 years. China has second largest economy (some claim largest already) after USA with increases of around 9.5% per annum. • The International Monetary Fund reports the country's GDP has increased considerably from just over $200 billion in 1980 to $5.9 trillion in 2010 although there are signs in 2012 of a slowdown. • 12th Five Year programme which is targeting economic growth (7% pa); more new jobs (45m urban areas) and price stability. • Inequalities have widened. China's Gini-coefficient has risen to 0.47, passing the USA 0.40, which is seen as high. Gap between town and country and coastal and inland regions. Average wages in cities are three times greater than rural wages. • A floating population of migrant workers with limited access to educational and health services for their families. • Since economic change has been introduced, hundreds of millions have been lifted out of poverty. There have been huge improvements in the standard of living for majority although millions continue to experience poverty including many in countryside and migrant workers, e.g. average urban disposable incomes are three times that of the average rural disposable income. • Range of policies to reduce rural poverty, curb pollution, improve health and education, etc.	
		Any other valid point that meets the criteria described in the general marking principles for this type of question.	
		Credit reference to aspects of the following — World Power: USA	
		• Relevant social/economic issues may include inequality, poverty, unemployment (around 9m), education, health, crime, etc. • American Recovery and Reinvestment Act (ARRA) • Affordable Care Act (2010) — more Americans have affordable/quality health care • Affirmative Action as operates in 2014 • Other policies to reduce poverty include EITC, TANF, food stamps, Child Care and Development Fund, Housing Choice Vouchers, etc. • Medicaid/Medicare/services for children — Free Health Care Social/Health Patient	
		Possible approaches to answering the question:	
		For a number of years the CPC leadership has been concerned about growing social and economic inequality. For example, urban incomes have grown at twice the rate of rural incomes. Although between 150–200m people have been lifted from absolute poverty, there are still anything up to 100m Chinese people who struggle to get enough to eat or have proper shelter.	
		(2 marks, one accurate point with exemplification)	

Question		Detailed marking principles	Max mark
2.	(b)	**(continued)** *In Deng's time as leader, getting rich was seen as 'glorious'. This view made economic development the priority and there was little concern for the resulting social or economic inequalities. However, under Presidents Zemin ('Socialism with Chinese characteristics'), Hu and more recently, Xi, the priority has been to promote economic, environmental and social development to achieve the 'Chinese Dream' and 'rejuvenate China'.* *In recent years, the CPC leadership had become acutely aware that if too many Chinese people were excluded from the general increase in wealth in society, this could result in serious social discontent. For example, it was reported by the Economist magazine that China has 2.3m millionaires in 2013 and yet there are also around 80m Chinese people living in extreme poverty. One consequence of the rise in social and economic inequality has been a rise in the number of popular protests (70,000+, 2013). By way of response, the CPC has introduced a number of poverty-reduction programmes.* ***(5 marks, one accurate point with extended explanation, detailed exemplification and evaluative comment)*** *Overall, China has had limited success in terms of tackling social and economic inequalities. For although many Chinese people have been lifted out of extreme poverty, the inequality gap between the richest and poorest has widened.* ***(1 mark, balanced overall comment that addresses the question)***	
	(c)	**Evaluate** **Credit responses that make reference to:** • A world issue and ways in which international organisations attempt to solve it. • Evaluation of the success of international organisations in resolving a world issue **Credit reference to aspects of the following:** • World issue: international terrorism • World issue: conflict, e.g. Middle East, Ukraine, Syria, Libya, Iraq, Afghanistan, North Korea, etc. • World issue: poverty in the developing world • World issue: nuclear proliferation • World issue: global economic crisis • Reference may be made to any international organisation including the United Nations (UN), North Atlantic Treaty Organisation (NATO), European Union (EU), African Union (AU), etc. or voluntary organisations such as Oxfam and Save the Children, etc. • Credit reference to ways in which international organisations can work to solve a world issue including diplomacy/international cooperation, use of aid/trade and sanctions, peace talks, peacekeeping troops, military intervention, etc. *Any other valid point that meets the criteria described in the general marking principles for this type of question* **Possible approaches to answering the question:** *Russian interference in Ukraine and Putin's Russian nationalism are of great concern to NATO and the EU. Both diplomatically (at G8 conferences) and economically (sanctions), western leaders have tried to pressurise Putin into changing Russian policy.* ***(2 marks, accurate and developed point)*** *Russia's interference in Ukraine and Putin's Russian nationalism are of great concern to NATO and the EU. In 2014, Russia encouraged unrest in Crimea which led to Crimea illegally leaving Ukraine and becoming part of Russia. Russia has also supported rebels in Eastern Ukraine, backing them with heavy arms and troops. Both diplomatically (at G8 conferences) and economically (sanctions), western leaders have tried to pressurise Putin into changing Russian policy. So far, however, Putin remains defiant although there are signs that the Russian economy is in trouble with currency revenues falling from reduced oil sales and the rouble under pressure.* ***(4 marks, accurate point with explanation, exemplification and evaluative comment)*** *Overall, it would appear that the response of NATO and EU to Russian aggression has not been a success. Some people argue that the economic sanctions imposed are too little, too late. Reality is that Russia has annexed Crimea and that Eastern Ukraine will almost certainly fall under Russian influence regardless of what NATO, the EU or the Ukrainian government says.* ***(2 marks, balanced overall comment that addresses the question)***	12

Question		Detailed marking principles	Max mark
2.	(d)	**Evaluate** **Credit responses that make reference to:** • Causes of a world issue • Evaluation of the importance of political problems as a cause of world issue **Credit reference to aspects of the following:** • World issue: international terrorism • World issue: conflict e.g. Middle East, Ukraine, Syria, Libya, Iraq, Afghanistan, North Korea, etc. • World issue: poverty in the developing world • World issue: nuclear proliferation • World issue: global economic crisis • Many world issues are primarily caused by poverty or inequality (socio-economic), others are more political, e.g. nuclear proliferation or authoritarian/undemocratic government. There is also conflict over land and self-determination, e.g. Israel/Palestine. **Possible approaches to answering the question:** *After fighting for independence for over 50 years South Sudan finally became independent in 2011 from Sudan. In this period over 2 million people were killed by fighting and starvation. The war in Sudan was a political and ethnic war between the Arab Moslem North and the mostly Black Christian South.* *(2 marks, accurate point with exemplification)* *Lack of development within many African countries is an important world issue. However, the reasons for the lack of development are complex and involve many different factors, including politics. For example, political and ethnic divisions between the rulers of South Sudan sparked the current civil war in the country. In 2013, the President Salva Kiir sacked the Vice- President Riek Machar over allegations of corruption, and armed conflict subsequently broke out. Mr Kiir belongs to the largest ethnic group, the Dinka, and Mr Machar to the Nuer. Since December 2013 more than a million people have fled their homes and there have been widespread mass killings along ethnic lines.* *(4 marks, accurate point with explanation, exemplification and evaluative comment)* *Lack of development within many African countries is an important world issue. However, the reasons for the lack of development are complex and involve many different factors, including politics. For example, political and ethnic divisions between the rulers of South Sudan sparked the current civil war in the country. In 2013, the President Salva Kiir sacked the Vice- President Riek Machar over allegations of corruption, and armed conflict subsequently broke out. Mr Kiir belongs to the largest ethnic group, the Dinka, and Mr Machar to the Nuer. Since December 2013, more than a million people have fled their homes, schools have closed, farms are deserted, there are massive food shortages and there have been widespread mass killings along ethnic lines.* *However, it is not only political instability that can cause a lack of development in Africa. The majority of African countries have large and unsustainable external debts. A report by the Ghanaian government in 2013 stated the country had an external debt of over $10,000m. There is no doubt the amount of external debt and the interest paid on these debts limits development in many African countries.* *(6 marks, accurate and developed point with extended explanation, detailed exemplification and evaluative comment)*	12

Acknowledgements

Permission has been sought from all relevant copyright holders and Hodder Gibson is grateful for the use of the following:

Source B: Charts adapted from 'National Voting Intention: the impact of the first debate – How would you vote if there were a General Election tomorrow' taken from 'General Election 2010, The Leaders' Debates, The worms' final verdict – lessons to be learned' 30 April 2010, by Ipsos Mori. Chart A: 'Before the first debate: 21-23 March' (Base: All certain to vote = 833 unweighted; data collected among 1,503 British adults 18+, 19th-22nd March 2010). Chart B: 'After the first debate:
18-19 April' (Base: All certain to vote = 802 unweighted; data collected among 1,253 British adults 18+, 18th-19th April 2010). Reproduced by kind permission of Ipsos MORI (SQP page 3);
Source B: 'General acute inpatient discharges with an alcohol-related diagnosis: Scotland' (http://www.scotland.gov.uk/Topics/Statistics/Browse/Health/TrendAlcohol) Source: Information Services Division (ISD) Scotland © NHS National Services Scotland (Model Paper 1 page 6);
Source C: 'Alcohol-related deaths rates per 100,000 of population (selected areas) 2012'. Adapted from data from the Office for National Statistics, licensed under the Open Government Licence v.2.0. (Model Paper 1 page 6);
Source A: 'Outstanding Victory for Obama in 2012 USA Presidential Elections'. Adapted from BBC News website November 2012 (http://www.bbc.co.uk/news/world-us-canada-20233064) (Model Paper 2 page 6);
Source B: 'Voting by age, income, religious affiliation and race in 2012 Presidential Election (%)' Source: Figures from the 2012 President Exit Polls by Edison Research for the National Election Pool, a consortium of ABC News, Associated Press, CBS News, CNN, FoxNews and NBC News (Model Paper 2 page 7);
Source C: 'US Presidential Results 2012: popular and electoral College (%)' Adapted from BBC News website November 2012 (Model Paper 2 page 8);
Source B: Figures taken from Huffpost Pollster (http://elections.huffingtonpost.com/pollster) (Model Paper 3 page 7).

Hodder Gibson would like to thank SQA for use of any past exam questions that may have been used in model papers, whether amended or in original form.